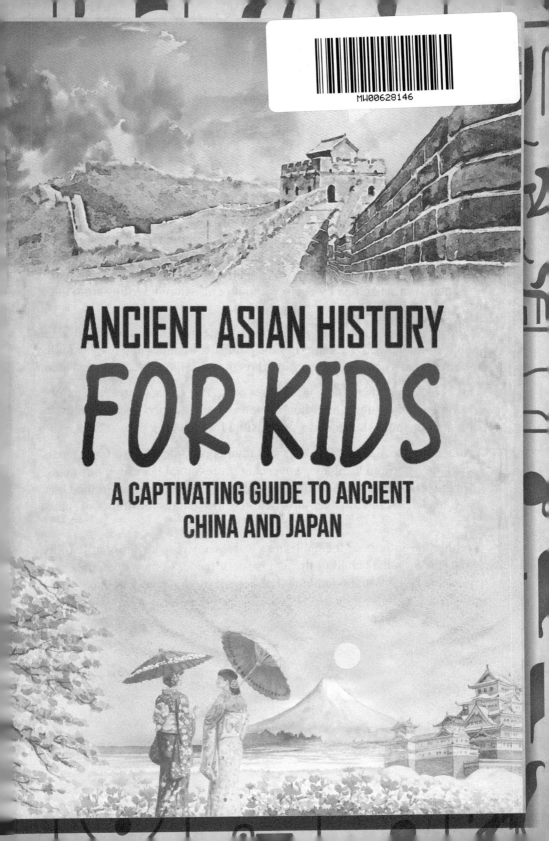

ANCIENT ASIAN HISTORY
FOR KIDS

A CAPTIVATING GUIDE TO ANCIENT CHINA AND JAPAN

Table of Contents

Part 1:
Ancient China for Kids

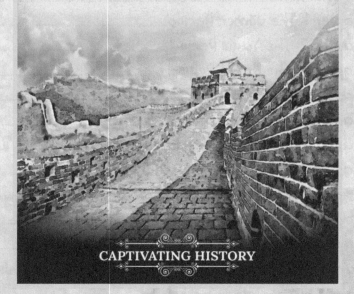

ANCIENT CHINA
FOR KIDS

A CAPTIVATING GUIDE TO ANCIENT CHINESE HISTORY, FROM THE SHANG DYNASTY TO THE FALL OF THE HAN DYNASTY

CAPTIVATING HISTORY

INTRODUCTION

Heroes, evil emperors, legends of men who fought against nine-headed snakes, and sorcerers that could tell the future are all here in this book. So why should you read this book?

History is fascinating. It teaches us not to make the same mistakes as those that came before us.

It shows us the power of the people who lived long ago and inspires us to be better.

This book is an in-depth look at the great history of Ancient China. From the Great Wall of China to inventing paper, Ancient China has been an important part of our world's development.

By picking up this book, you are giving yourself the gift of reading information that is not only interesting but real, too. How cool is that!

The Yellow River Valley

Imagine a time without Nintendo Switch and Pokémon. I know it is hard, or maybe even impossible to do, but thousands of years ago, people lived without all the fun and convenient things we have that make our lives so easy today. People lived off the land because it was all they had. They made their pottery, clothes, homes, and they hunted for food themselves. Most of us have watched some surviva shows on TV, but let me tell you, these people were the original rea survivors.

The Yellow River Valley was where ancient Chinese civilizations started. It is often called "Mother River" because civilizations were born here, two in particular: the Yangshao and Longshan cultures. The river has played an important part in Ancient China. We will learn more about all the people who lived in the areas around the river. It was their home, and it gave them food, water, and materials.

The Yangshao Culture

During the final stage of the stone age, a small civilization started along the Yellow River Valley called the Yangshao Culture. The Yangshao Culture dated from 5000 BCE to 3000 BCE; now, that is quite some time ago! Let's read about how they lived.

Food

The Yangshao Culture couldn't just push a few buttons on their phones and have an UberEATS driver bring them their favorite meals. When they were hungry, they needed to search for their food. They mostly lived on millet and rice, and enjoyed the rich river soil. However, when the earth became overused, they packed up their belongings and moved to a new spot down the river. Can you imagine having to pack up all your belongings today just to move a few meters down the street? That was a way of life for the Yangshao Culture. They kept pigs and dogs, and on occasion, cows, sheep, and goats. If they wanted to eat meat instead of millet and rice, they caught fish from the river. They used stone tools to catch fish.

Houses

The Yangshao Culture used clay, mud, poles made from trees, and millet stalks to build their houses. They built a pen outside for animals. The houses were simple, but it was a safe place for people to rest after a long day after working outside.

Crafts

The Yangshao culture made pottery, and they decorated it with fine white, red, and black paint. They loved painting their faces, animals, and shapes on their pottery. We can still see some of their pottery in Chinese museums today.

They also made silk and wove hemp. This was used to make loincloths for the men. The woman wore a cloth around their bodies.

Now before we jump into the Longshan culture, it is joke time!

Why is a History book like a fruit cake? It is full of dates.

Dates! Get it? Come on, that's funny!

The Longshan Culture

After the Yangshao culture, the Longshan culture existed from about 3000 BCE. They are sometimes called the Black Pottery Culture. Can you guess why? Yes, they mastered black pottery making - but more about that later. They lived in the middle and lower Yellow River valley areas. Let's learn more about them.

THE LONGSHAN CULTURE

Yangshao map Credit: Kanguole
https://commons.wikimedia.org/wiki/
File:Yangshao_map.svg

5

Food

They enjoyed millet, rice, and wheat, and their favorite source of meat was pigs. They started herding animals, and they had chickens, pigs, dogs - and sometimes cattle. The Longshan culture loved growing plants and crops, and they used the river's fertile soil very well. They had a much more exciting diet than the Yangshao culture because they were smart about using the land.

Crafts

Yangshao artifacts
https://www.flickr.com/photos/101561334@N08/103394848864/

They produced some silk by keeping silkworms, but they are most remembered for their black pottery. Their pottery was beautiful and can still be seen today. Not all their pottery was black. At times they also made grey and white pottery. They made cooking pots and egg shelling pots. What are egg shelling pots, you might ask? If you guessed that they are pots used for shelling eggs, then you are right!

Tongue twister challenge! Can you say this three times fast without getting your tongue twisted? The Longshan culture made egg shelling pots to shell eggs. Could you do it?

Longshan weapons
https://commons.wikimedia.org/wiki/File:Longshan_Culture_Stone_Weapons.jpg

Houses

The Longshan culture lived in houses made the same way as the Yangshao culture. In fact, these two cultures lived very much the same way. The biggest difference was that the Longshan culture was much more focused on growing crops, and their pottery skills were better. The Longshan culture also made more tools, especially for planting rice and grinding wheat. Having more tools made it easier for them to plant their seeds better. That resulted in better crops and happier people with full bellies.

What problems did these cultures face?

Both cultures were lucky to live off a river as rich and fertile as the Yellow River, but this had a downside. Jealous tribes would often come to take what wasn't theirs. They would attack the cultures, stealing their animals, food, and tools. Now that's just mean. So, the people had to learn to stand together and fight back against these bullying tribes. After all, many people are much more powerful than one. This was hard to get used to since everyone wanted to take charge. After some time and more annoying tribe attacks, it became clear that the cultures needed a leader, someone who told, while the others followed. That became the first rise of the ancient Chinese civilization's single tribe leader. The leader was a shaman-chief that led the people through hardships. When he died, the shaman-chief was surrounded by dragon and tiger figures that the people had made from clamshells.

The tiger and dragon figures were meant to protect the shaman-chief in the afterlife. Who would bother you if you had tigers and dragons by your side? Many decades later, these dragon and tiger figures were found in a small area that had been a Yangshao village.

Another uncontrollable problem they faced was floods. Flooding was a big problem for the cultures because it meant losing their homes and crops and often their belongings. Once again, this was just a way of life for the people of the Yangshao and Longshan cultures. Nature gave, and sometimes Nature took. All they could do was save what they could and start again with what they had. After a flood, they would take what could still be used and move to a new area along the river. Luckily for them, the river was always a reliable friend.

What can we learn from them?

The Yangshao and Longshan cultures were creative, hardworking, and tough. They faced lots of challenges, but they never gave up. Just like them, we also face challenges in our lives at times. So, stay strong, and never give up because you are a true survivor like the Yangshao and Longshan cultures!

The First Dynasty

Now we move on to something so mythical that it is only spoken about in legends. In 2070 BCE, The Xia Dynasty was founded by Yu the Great, a legendary ruler of ancient China. It was the first dynasty in traditional Chinese history. Before the Western Zhou dynasty (which was more than 1000 years later), there was no information about the Xia dynasty. So people started to believe that it was just a mystical legend, and that Yu was changed into human form for our history.

Yu the Great
https://en.wikipedia.org/wiki/Yu_the_Great#/media/
File:King_Yu_of_Xia.jpg

Before the Xia dynasty, it was a time called The Three Sovereigns and Five Emperors. Three demigods (half-god, half-human) ruled over the lands, with five emperors being their human helpers. One of the five emperors who helped the demigods was called Emperor Zhuanxu. He had a son, Gun, who had another son, Yu. Emperor Zhuanxu's grandson would grow up to be Yu, the Great.

Yu grew up in the mountains surrounding the yellow river. The river was constantly flooding, and people were tired of the damage. One of the five emperors asked Yu's father to find the solution to this problem. Yu's father tried his best to solve this problem for nine long years, but the flooding continued. Finally, he built dams to gather the water, but one of his dams collapsed, and people got hurt. The emperor was furious and imprisoned Yu's father for his failure.

The river flooding was now Yu's problem to fix. Instead of being scared or angry because of what happened to his dad, Yu was determined to learn from his father's mistakes. He organized tribes from all over the region to build a system that would flow the water out to sea. Yu became a confident builder over the years and started building amazing dams and canals all over China. He gave the tribes a new purpose. Yu was very popular among the tribes because he would work - and even eat and sleep -with them. This made them love him and motivated them to give him their best. He was a great leader because he saw himself as one of the people.

Yu's projects to improve the land took thirteen years to complete. During that time, the tribes adored him - even worshipped him. He was the one they had been waiting for.

There are stories about Yu's bravery. It is said that Yu defeated a nine-headed snake with the help of a yellow dragon and a black turtle. Now that is a fierce battle! It's believed that he did so much for the land and the people that the gods offered him special help. He traveled through China while sitting on the back of a 10,000-year-old turtle. I hope it was a fast turtle. Some believe that the river gods gave him maps of rivers, and he cleared entire channels in the mountains with his mighty ax.

Yu's hard work was so excellent that he was seen as a superhuman. He was a very dedicated builder. For thirteen years, he worked across the land. He didn't return to his home to his wife once during that time. He passed his front door three times in the thirteen years, but he never went in. He didn't even turn back when his young son saw him for the first time and called out his name. He dug mud day after day, year after year, until the job was done. He was unstoppable.

Temple of Yu The Great
https://commons.wikimedia.org/wiki/File:Temple_of_Yu_the_Great_in_Shaoxing,_Zhejiang,_China.jpg

Yu Becomes Emperor Yu

One of the five emperors, Emperor Shun, was amazed by the wonderful structures that Yu had built and how the tribes adored him. He was so impressed that he offered to pass the throne to Yu even though he had a son who was supposed to take over the throne. At first, Yu refused to take the throne, but with the  community behind him, he changed his mind and took his place as Emperor Yu when he was 33 years old. That was when the Xia dynasty was born.

Yu was a very popular and good emperor, and he took great care of his people. Yu ruled for 45 years and passed the throne to his son, Qi, when he died while hunting. Yu was such a legendary figure that he is one of the few Chinese leaders that carry the title "Great."

The End of The Xia Dynasty

After Yu died, the throne was passed from emperor to emperor. The dynasty started to weaken until it was ruled by Emperor Jie, in 1600 BCE, who was mean and hard on the people. Emperor Jie was soon overthrown by King Tang, who was the first king of the Shang Dynasty.

Riddle challenge! Can you solve this riddle?

It is a place with lots of history
It includes the Ming Dynasty
Shanghai is the largest city
Art and pottery are found a plenty
What country is it?

Answer: China

The Almighty Emperor Tang

Emperor Tang was the Chinese emperor who overthrew the horrible Emperor Jie. Emperor Tang founded the Shang Dynasty in 1600 BCE.

It is said that Tang was the great-grandson of the mythical sage-king, Huangdi, the Yellow Emperor. Legends tell us that Tang read about the evil ruler Jie on the shell of a tortoise, and he knew he had to step up and claim the dynasty.

Tang was a great and generous leader to his people who always offered whatever he could to make sure they were happy. It is said that a drought made his people unhappy because all of their crops died. Determined to end the drought at any cost, Tang offered himself to the heavens, and it started to rain heavily, saving the people and their leader. In drawings of Tang, he is shown as at least 9 feet tall, with a white face and whiskers. He had a very pointed head and arms that were six-jointed. What a magnificent emperor!

The Birth of the Bronze Age

As the Shang Dynasty continued to strengthen, the Chinese Bronze Age began around 1700 BCE along the banks of the Yellow River. Although the Shang kings who came after Tang ruled areas much larger than that, their attention stayed on the yellow river and the development of this wonderful Bronze Age.

Weapons and Tools

The Bronze Age was a very exciting time when men learned how to make bronze weapons and tools by mining and smelting copper. Bronze is much harder and lasts longer than copper, so soon, people were learning how to make all of their tools and weapons out of Bronze. To make weapons and tools, the people needed skilled artisans. They would develop the best weapons and tools they could by learning and experimenting with what the Yellow River gave them.

Before the Bronze Age started, people made their tools using stone, and they hunted with spears. With the Bronze Age, they had the chance to learn how to farm to have more food to feed others who offered them a service. They could get the help of miners, smiths, weavers, potters, and builders who lived in the small towns by feeding them.

Years after the Shang Dynasty ended, ruins of old music instruments were found. This tells us that the Shang people

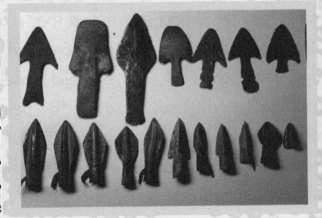

were curious about music, and they made many different instruments using copper.

Food

We often believe that they drank tea and ate rice, but this isn't true. Rice and tea came from the south, and the Yellow River didn't care much for either until hundreds of years later. The people of the Bronze Age enjoyed eating cereals, bread, and cakes made of millet and barley. They drank beer. Those who could afford it added meat and wine to their meals.

The First Chinese Scripts

The people were not only farming and making bronze tools and weapons, but they also started writing. Using oracle bones made of animal bones or parts of a turtle's shell, people started engraving, which was the earliest form of Chinese writing. The Shang people wrote on these oracle bones to talk to their ancestors. They believed their ancestors had the power to give them fortune and keep disasters away from them. They also thought that their ancestors gave them guidance that would make them successful and keep them healthy. The sky also guided the people as they believed their ancestors hid messages within the stars, so they started with the Shang calendar.

Early Chinese writing (Shang Dynasty oracle bones)
https://www.flickr.com/photos/101561334@N08/9830601816

The Bronze Age Chinese had powerful ideas about what made a strong leader, and they believed the king had to have the best relationship with his ancestors. Therefore, those ancestors controlled his kingdom's success. Kings were encouraged to communicate with their ancestors, often using oracle bones. To get an answer from the ancestors, a priest held a hot rod to the bone until it cracked, and then he interpreted the pattern of the cracks for the ancestors' answers.

Bronze coins

Before the time of the Shang Dynasty, people traded what they needed using shell money. Yes, shells were used as money. Can you imagine buying your favorite candy bar with a handful of shells today? When the Bronze Age came, the people started making bronze coins for trading. This was the beginning of using coins as money, something that we are still using today.

Early Chinese currency (Shang cowrie coins)
https://commons.wikimedia.org/wiki/File:005_Xia_or_Shang_Bone_Cowrie_Money.jpg

The Shang Kings' Duties

The king's responsibility was to keep the city safe, so the Shang kings spent most of their time riding around their cities with their nobles and knights to hunt and fight wars. The kings appointed people who would oversee the farmers since they were peasants who belonged to the land.

The Shang people believed that the sun and rain gods controlled the harvest. Therefore, it was the king's duty to keep them happy. If the rain and sun gods gave the Shang Dynasty good harvests, they would show their thanks by placing wine and cereal in specially made bronze bowls and heat them over a fire at an altar.

The End of the Shang Dynasty

Around the year 1046 BCE, the Shang Dynasty was ruled by an evil and cruel king, King Di Xin, who didn't care for his people. The Shang people were unhappy. Conquerors from Zhou wanted to defeat the evil king because heaven told them the horrible king's ruling had to end.

A powerful leader of the Zhou, a state of the Shang Dynasty, named Wen Wang knew it would be up to him to make the suffering stop. He had to take over from the evil king. It took many years, but finally, his son, Wu Wang, led an army across the Yellow River and defeated the evil King Di Xin. King Wu established a new dynasty known as the Zhou Dynasty.

The end of King Di Xin's reign would become a message to all emperors for years to come. Be good to your people, Kings, or a better king will step in and take your place.

Chapter 4: The Zhou Dynasty

The Longest Dynasty

The Zhou Dynasty was founded in 1046, and it became the longest dynasty in the history of Chinese dynasties, stretching to 256 BCE. It was not just the longest dynasty but also the most important when it comes to Chinese culture. The Zhou Dynasty was divided into two periods. Western Zhuo lasted from 1046 to 771 BCE, and Eastern Zhou lasted from 771 to 256 BCE.

The Zhou Dynasty believed in the king's ruling above all else, which led to them inventing the Mandate of Heaven. The Mandate of Heaven stated that the heavens sent the kings and that there could be only one king to rule China, one king to rule over all the nobles. It would be used to justify the rule of one emperor ever since.

The Iron Age

The Zhou people were using bronze in better ways than ever before. They were fantastic at smelting metals at high temperatures and hammering them until they made perfect tools and weapons. At the end of the Shang Dynasty, bronze was still mostly used, but people started using iron as the Zhou Dynasty grew and developed. For example, they used meteoric iron, iron from meteors that crashed into Earth very long ago. Now that is out of this world!

The Western Zhou

The first half of the Zhou Dynasty was the Western Zhou. The people were masters of weapon making. They made many weapons, including swords, spears, bows, war chariots, and shields for defending themselves in battle. Their most impressive weapon was a dagger axe. It was the weapon every soldier carried. These weapons made it possible for them to protect their land and their people against tribal attacks. The people could farm happily, knowing that their crops will be protected.

Western Zhou bronze fittings (tigers) Credit: Mary Harrsch
tps://www.flickr.com/photos/mharrsch/19912564642/in/photostream/

The early years of Western Zhou were very successful, with the people growing in knowledge and power. However, this only lasted about 75 years. The dynasty created a system of order that would help the king reign over the growing land. It was known as the Feng jian policy, and the power ran in this order:

- King
- Nobles (people with noble birth)
- Gentries (Upper-class people)
- Merchants (people who sold or traded goods)
- Laborers (workers)
- Peasants (people of low status)

Every noble formed his own little state with its own legal system, tax code, money, and army. However, every state still had to respect the king's ruling. They had to pay taxes to the king and give him their soldiers whenever he asked. The Fengjian policy was very successful, and the dynasty flourished. This was one of the few times in the history of Ancient China that the upper and lower classes worked together for the greater common good. But, unfortunately, the peaceful time could not last. The king was slowly losing control over the people because they wanted to be free to do as they please without a king's ruling. It got worse and worse until, in 771 BCE, the Zhou were forced out of the Yellow River valley, and King You of Zhou was killed. The people had taken control of the land.

The Eastern Zhou

Eastern Zhou bronze yi and pan Credit: Gary Todd
https://upload.wikimedia.org/wikipedia/common
s/c/c0/Eastern_Zhou_Bronze_Yi_%26_Pan.jpg

After the fall of Western Zhou, it was the beginning of the Eastern Zhou. This era lasted 515 years, and 25 kings in that time ruled the dynasty in that time. The Eastern Zhou was divided into two periods. The first half of the dynasty was called the Spring and Autumn

Period. The second half of the Eastern Zhou Dynasty was called the Warring States period.

The Spring and Autumn Period

When the Eastern Zhou Dynasty started, there was a period called the Spring and Autumn Period. Although the name sounds quite peaceful and friendly, it was a time full of battles and conflict. The people were fighting against the idea of one king for all. Instead, they wanted the states of the dynasty to have their own power.

After the capital of Zhengzhou was attacked by a group of non-Chinese tribals, the Zhou moved the capital east so that it would be close to the people who would support it. However, they waited too long. By that time, it was already too late for the Zhou. There were four mighty states known as Qin, Jin, Qi, and Chu. They already started fighting together against the one king rule.

Along with the battles and the fighting, this period was a great time for music, poetry, and philosophy in Ancient China's history. This was

the time of Confucius, Sun Tzu, and Lao Tzu and their teachings.

Eastern Zhou royal chariot pit Credit: Gary Todd
https://commons.wikimedia.org/wiki/File:Eastern_Zhou_Royal_Chariot
_Pit_Luoyang_17.jpg

This period was not a peaceful time at all. In fact, it was filled with battles over dominance. However, in the end, it was the Qin state that won, and it became the first Chinese state. The other state rulers looked up to the Qin state and followed its example. They all declared themselves king of their own states, ending the one king rule. With each state ruled by its own leader, the states improved in family, philosophy, and the arts.

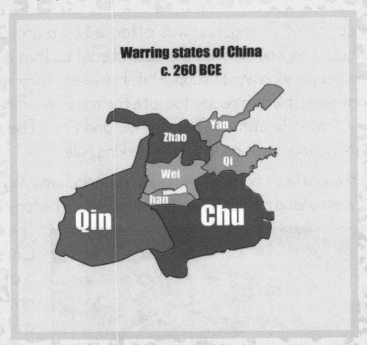

Warring states of China c. 260 BCE

Between 535 and 286 BCE, there was a lot of conflict between the states, and 358 wars took place. That's a crazy number for wars, right? The battle started yet again. The prize that everyone wanted was to be the one ruler of all of China. King Zhao of Qin defeated King Nan of Zhou and conquered West Zhou in 256 BCE. His grandson, King Zhuangxiang of Qin, conquered East Zhou. The Zhou Dynasty had come to an end.

The First Imperial Dynasty

The Qin Dynasty was the first empire in China. The empire existed from 221 to 206 BCE, which is not a long time at all. However, it had a great impact on Chinese culture.

The First Emperor of Qin

Qin Shi Huang was the first emperor of Qin, and the dynasty was named after him. Qin had big plans for China. He started to improve his military so that he could seize the five states around Qin. He did this in 221 BCE, and a unified Chinese empire was born.

Qin Shi Huang
https://en.wikipedia.org/wiki/File:Qinshihuang.jpg

Qin Shi Huang was a strong leader who wouldn't stop until he had everyone under his will. He organized 36 command areas on the land and assigned a governor, a military commander, and an imperial inspector to each. They all had to report back to him. He moved important families to the capital, Xianyang, so that he could keep an eye on them. He divided the lands into 36 command areas, each supervised by a governor, a military commander, and an imperial inspector, all of whom reported to him. He truly was ruling over everyone. People's weapons were taken and melted down.

Qin Shi Huang did a lot for the people, too. He made new currency, simplified weights and measurements. This meant that his people could trade using only one currency and use one weight system. This made things a lot easier for everyone. He ordered his men to build wagon axles of a specific size so that they could fit nicely on the roads. It is always better to drive in something that fits on the roads, isn't it?

The Simple Script

The area that Qin Shi Huang conquered was home to many different cultures and languages. So he knew he had to work hard to bring everyone together. He started with a standard written script that all his people could use. The script was simple, so it made it easy for people to write quickly. People liked it because they could keep records faster than ever before. The fantastic thing about the script was that it made it possible for people who didn't speak the same language to communicate using writing. Although he encouraged his people to write, he looked at everything that they wrote. If he didn't like what they wrote, he would burn their work. Imagine your teacher burning your homework. As the years passed, he became more controlling, even sentencing the writer to death if he disagreed with their books.

The Great Wall
Credit: Peter Dowley https://www.flickr.com/photos/pedronet/2639612640

Buildings and Construction

Qin had thousands of men under his command. He divided them into two groups. One group had to defend his land against the tribes of the south. The other group had to build palaces, canals, and roads. Qin wanted to have the largest palace in the world. So he ordered his builders to build the E Pang Palace. They started building it in 212 BCE, but it was so big that they only finished the front of it when he died. So he never saw his precious palace.

He ordered his men to build irrigation systems all over the land. He also wanted to keep his land safe from attacks. So he created 44 small cities surrounded by walls overlooking the river. He was defending a line of 3000 miles. It was a tough project, and many of his workers died. Some died because they got injured, and some died because they were just too tired. This led him to begin the Great Wall of China and the Terracotta Soldiers.

The Secret Life of Qin

Terracotta Army:
Credit: Güldem Üstün https://www.flickr.com/photos/guldem/26279806738

Qin Shi Huang had a stressful life. A sorcerer Lu Sheng warned him of his safety. Qin started traveling through secret tunnels and lived in secret places. His people were not allowed to use his name on any documents. Anyone who shared his location would face their death. He wanted to live forever. He ordered his advisors to find herbs that would make him live forever. Of course, they never did. He was so dedicated to living forever that he ordered his men to make an army of terracotta soldiers to be buried with him when he died. The soldiers were meant to protect him in the afterlife.

End of the Qin Dynasty

Qin Shi Huang died in 210 BCE, and his young son became the new emperor. This didn't go well. Two years later, most of the empire was fighting against the new emperor. Warlord Xiang Yu battled against the Qin army and won. He killed the emperor, destroyed the capital, and divided the empire into 18 states.

Liu Bang was leading the Han River Valley. He battled against other kings and then fought against Xiang Yu for three years. Finally, in 202 BCE Xiang Yu died. Lin Bang became the emperor of the Han Dynasty.

The Second Imperial Dynasty

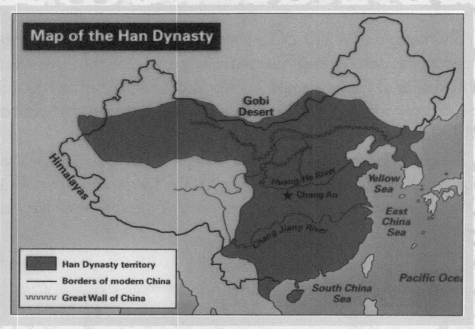

Han Dynasty map
https://www.china-mike.com/wp-content/uploads/2011/01/Han-dynasty-Map.jpg

The second Imperial Dynasty of China was the Han Dynasty. The Han Dynasty ruled China from 206 BCE to 220 AD. The people of Qin were still mourning the death of emperor Qin Sin Huang when warlord Xiang Yu took control for a short time. Finally, it was emperor Liu Bang who took control of the Han Dynasty in 202 BCE.

Western Han

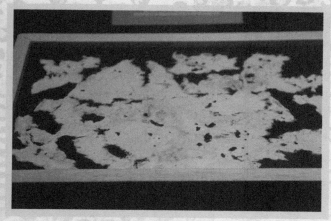

Liu Bang established the Han capital of Chang'an. It was along the Wei River. Although most of the Qin Dynasty's palaces have been destroyed, there was one that stood perfectly. Liu Bang moved into the palace and changed his name to Emperor Gaozu. The period of Western Han started and lasted until 23 AD.

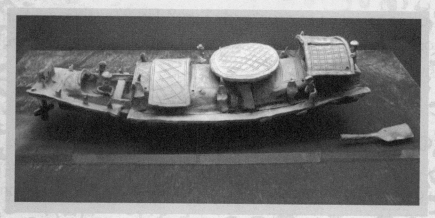

Gaozu didn't want any more battles for dominance, so he replaced the kings of the surrounding kingdoms with members of his own family before he died in 195 BCE. The joke was on Gaozu because his family members had plans of their own.

Empress Lu Zhi

After Gaozu died, Empress Lu Zhi tried to take control by killing some of Gaozu's sons. Lu Zhi would stop at nothing to be in complete control. She even killed her mother. The three kings who ruled after Gaozu were puppet kings. Empress Lu Zhi controlled them. She was finally the one with the power. She was so feared that no one would stand up to her. Could you imagine someone so cruel and scary? The struggle went on for 15 years before one of Gaozu's sons, Wan, killed her entire family and became emperor.

Wang Mang and the New Dynasty

In 9AD, the Western Han ended when Wang Mang seized the throne. The last several emperors had died young, and their power had mostly gone to their uncles. Wang broke this tradition by declaring "The New Dynasty."

Wang Mang believed in giving back to the people. Much like a Chinese Robin Hood, he took from the rich and gave to the poor. He took wealthy estates and gave them to the peasants. Everything seemed to go very well for the New Dynasty, but it was just the calm before the storm. In 23 AD, there was a huge flood. The peasants were angry, and they started a group called the

Red Eyebrows. They called themselves the Red Eyebrows because they painted their eyebrows red before battle. This group killed Wang Mang and destroyed Chang'an.

The grandson of Gaozu, Liu Xiu, took over as emperor. He established the Eastern Han Dynasty.

Eastern Han

Emperor Liu Xiu was weak, and the Red Eyebrows killed him within two years of his reign. It was Emperor Guangwu who took control of Eastern Han. He had many plans to prevent the chaos of the Xin Dynasty from happening again. He set firm rules for everyone and moved the capital to Luoyang, where he could keep an eye on it.

The Han Dynasty became strong under the leadership of Guangwu. However, the emperors who followed Guangwu didn't care about the people at all. The third emperor, Huan, is said to have been so lazy that he would arrest anyone who gave him more work. The Eastern Han was weakening because of bad leadership. The people lost faith in the emperors. The Han was trying to expand to Vietnam and Korea. These efforts were costly. People grew even more unhappy when they were forced to pay higher taxes. They began to hate their emperor, and he stood alone.

Emperor Lingdi took over from Huan, and the people struggled with floods and hunger. With the Han at its weakest, Warlord Cao started a war to gain complete control of China. Although he was defeated, the country was divided up into three kingdoms. They were Cao Wei, Eastern Wu, and Shu Han. They each claimed the Mandate of Heaven, and that was the end of the Han Dynasty. The Six Dynasties Period followed the Han, a time that would transform China.

The Han Dynasty was so much more than just years of battles and wars. It was a time where people were learning and growing very much. The dynasty improved their schools so that their people could be educated. The Han Dynasty was also a time where art blossomed. Most of the art came from tombs of important families. We can still see The Wu Family site today. It is two

underground chambers under four shrines. The tomb has 70 carved stones, painted ceilings, and walls with paintings of historical people.

Han board game
https://images.metmuseum.org/CRDImages/as/original/DP372026.jpg

The site contained about 3,000 Han Dynasty art figures made of silver, bronze, gold, jade, silk, and pottery.

The Han developed music theory and invented the seismometer - that's a tool used to detect and record earthquakes! It also invented paper and the waterwheel. The people were inspired - improving on the calendar, mathematics, cartography (the drawing and studying of maps), metallurgy (the science of metal), architecture, and astronomy. The Han Dynasty also created the Silk Road, a trade route that created a direct link to the West.

The Ancient Chinese were heroes when it came to inventions and technology. Many of these inventions changed the entire world and are still helpful today. This ancient culture made such an impact on our everyday life, that they are thanked for making the Four Great Inventions. These are the inventions that allowed our human race to evolve to where we are today. The four inventions are paper, gunpowder, the compass, and printing. However, China did so much more for us than those four inventions. Let's look at those – and all the other amazing inventions China has given us.

Silk Road landscape
Credit: fdecomite https://www.flickr.com/photos/fdecomite/4367669018

Traditional Chinese silk Credit: sergeant killjoy
https://www.flickr.com/photos/doc_bosco/2085169813

Silk is a very popular material around the world because it is soft and light. In 138 BCE, Emperor Wu sent a man named Zhang Qian to contact tribes to the west. The Xiongnu tribe captured him and his party, but Zhang Qian escaped and continued west. He reached the area we now know as Afghanistan, which was called Bactria at the time. There, he saw bamboo and Chinese textiles, but he was confused about how they got there. The people of Bactria told him it came from a kingdom called Shendu. In fact, what Zhang Qian didn't know was that silk had been found in Ancient Egypt, Rome, and the whole of Levant (the region along the eastern Mediterranean shores).

Zhang Qian explored the area for 13 years. Then he went back to his emperor. He told the emperor about Shendu and drew maps of how to get there. The maps were used more and more, resulting in the international trade route called Silk Road. Thanks to Zhang Qian, it was now possible for China to trade with Europe.

The Chinese learned how to make silk from the cocoons of silkworms, something they kept secret for hundreds of years. After China has been using silkworms for hundreds of years, Europe also started with the practice. Today silk is available everywhere.

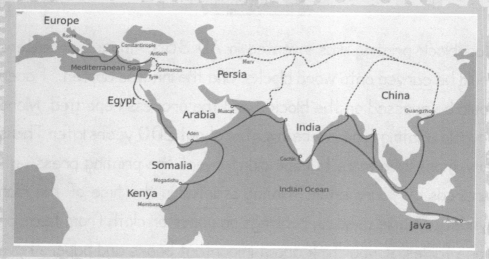

Silk Road map trail
Credit: Belsky https://commons.wikimedia.org/wiki/File:Silk_Road.svg

Paper

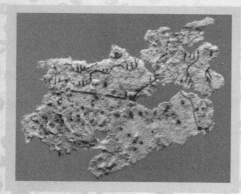

Ancient Chinese paper
https://commons.wikimedia.org/wiki/File:Fangmatan
_paper_map.jpg

The Chinese invented paper and many uses for it. These uses included paper money and playing cards. Can you imagine our lives without those two things? It sure is hard to do. Paper was invented in China during the Han Dynasty by Cai Lun around AD 105.

This inventor pounded ingredients like bamboo, hemp, rags, fishing nets, and mulberry tree bark into a pulp. Then he mixed it in water and spread it flat. The use of paper spread quickly through the empire, and so began people's love of paper.

Printing

Woodblock printing was invented in AD 868. Images or letters would be carved onto wood blocks, and the ink was applied. Paper would be pressed on the blocks, and the process repeated. More movable printing types were invented about 200 years later. This is very impressive since Europe didn't invent the printing press until hundreds of years later. Printing started in the time of the Han Dynasty. People used ink rubbings on paper or cloth from texts on stone tables. If you think about important books and papers have been in history, it's easy to understand why printing is considered as one of the Four Great Inventions of China!

The Compass

Have you ever been lost? It's not a fun experience. The Ancient Chinese didn't like it either. In fact, they disliked it so much that they found a way to avoid it. The Chinese invented the magnetic compass to help find the correct direction. They used this in city planning at first, but it became very important to map makers and ships' navigation.

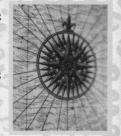

Gunpowder

Chemists invented gunpowder in the 9th century. It is said that they were trying to find the Elixir of Immortality. Soon after, engineers learned that gunpowder has military uses such as bombs, guns, mines, and even rockets. They also invented fireworks and made great beautiful firework displays for celebrations. We still use fireworks today to celebrate big occasions.

Boat Rudders

It was difficult to steer large ships in Ancient China. The rudder - usually a wood piece that hung down below the water to help guide the boat - was invented to help lead these large ships more quickly. The rudder made it possible for the Chinese to build massive ships in AD 200, years before Europe started building them! Boat rudders are still used today, making it possible to steer large ships that would otherwise be nearly impossible to move.

The Umbrella

We have all had a day where we got stuck in the rain. As our clothes, shoes, and bag got wet, we wished we remembered our umbrella! If you had to guess how long umbrellas have been around, what would you say? If your answer was more than 2 million days, you would be correct. The umbrella was first invented in 3500 BCE by the Chinese. Just like today, the Chinese used umbrellas to keep them from getting soaking wet when it rained. They also used the umbrella to keep them safe from the sun. Remember, they didn't have any sunblock back then! The Ancient Chinese used bamboo and oil-paper to make their umbrellas.

Porcelain

Porcelain is not just something pretty that Grandma puts her Sunday bakes on. It is an invention that changed the future of art around the world. The story of porcelain dates back to Eastern Han. The people heated ceramic materials to a high enough temperature to create porcelain. Porcelain is very durable, and we can still see pieces that they made in Eastern Han on display today. Although the porcelain is older than 2000 years old, it is still very colorful.

The Wheelbarrow

The wheelbarrow was invented in China by a man named Chuk Liang in the first century. He was tired of having too much to carry around. So he created the wheelbarrow to make his chores easier to do. Wheelbarrows make so many people's lives easier, and it is more popular than ever before. The design of the wheelbarrow hasn't changed in 1,700 years. Now, that is amazing.

Iron Casting

About 300 BCE, ironworkers in China discovered that burning iron ore makes a thick metallic liquid mixed with charcoal. This led them to invent cast iron. The hot liquid was poured into a mold that cools into hard, durable cast iron. Cast iron became an important part of Chinese life. The Chinese were making 150,000 tons a year before Europe even started making cast iron.

Hot Air Balloons

Have you ever been in a hot air balloon and wondered how it came to be? During the Three Kingdoms era, China invented the hot air balloon. The Chinese made Kongming lanterns that were lanterns that flew into the air unmanned. They used them to send signals to the military. These lanterns spread across Asia, and you can still see them today during the Loi Krathong Festival in Thailand.

Seismographs

The Chinese invented the first seismograph, or earthquake detector, in AD 132. The ancient seismometer (pronounced "size-mom-metter") was built with a large bronze bowl with eight dragon heads holding bronze balls. During an earthquake, the earth's movement would make a ball fall, showing the direction of the quake. So, hold onto your socks and hat whenever those dragons start dropping balls!

The Kite

About 3,000 years ago, the Chinese invented kites during the Han Dynasty. The first kite was made of silk and wood, and a farmer flew it. He tied a piece of silk to a string and then tied the line to his hat! The Chinese used kites to send messages - since they didn't have smartphones like we do.

Later the Chinese military attached bamboo pipes to their kites. As the kites flew over their enemies, the wind passed through the pipes, causing a whistling sound. The noise caused the troops to panic and run away. Imagine armies of strong men running from a kite! Kites came in many fantastic shapes, sizes, and bright colors. You could find kites shaped like birds, butterflies, tadpoles, and dragons. What kind of kite would you choose?

Matches

Matches are handy tools if you ever go on a camping trip. Did you know that the Chinese were the first people to invent matches?

Matches were invented during the kingdom of Northern Ch'i in AD 577. The Chinese used sticks and pine wood to make the first matches. So, don't forget every time you strike a match: you are using a Chinese invention.

The Fishing Rod

An ancient painting showed the existence of the fishing rod in China. The first fishing reel was also invented in China. This was thanks to the Yellow river. The river has always been an inspiration for the people of Ancient China, driving them to get better tools to fish.

Acupuncture

Acupuncture (placing needles into skin to help with pain and illnesses) treatment has been around since 6000 BCE, and people used long and sharp bones to do the treatments. Today's treatments are far less scary. Acupuncture is very useful and has many benefits for the body.

Abacus

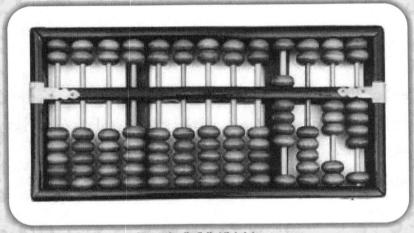

Abacus Credit: Felix Winkelnkemper
https://www.flickr.com/photos/winkelnkemper/47593100081

People in China first made an abacus about 2,500 years ago. An abacus is a very helpful math tool. In a way, it was the first computer that was ever invented. We can still use an abacus today to solve addition, subtraction, and multiplication problems. Many kids see the Abacus as a toy, but it is so much more than that; it has so many benefits!

Let's look at what an Abacus can do for you:

- It can help with concentration
- It can improve your listening and visual skills
- It can give you a better imagination
- It can help your memory improve
- It can help with your speed and accuracy
- It can boost your creativity
- It can increase your self-confidence

That is a long list of benefits. You can still find these in stores, so get yours and start enjoying this Ancient Chinese tool.

The I Ching

There is a book that is known as the world's oldest oracle (a message given by a prophet). It is the I Ching. It has helped people for generations. We can still buy the I Ching today. It is a fantastic collection of pictures, poetry, and advice. The I Ching is very simple to use. All you need is a copy of the book and three coins.

First, you toss the coins and let them fall six times. A "heads" is worth three, while a "tails" is only worth two. After your six attempts, add up the totals. If your total is an even number, draw a broken line (- -). If your total number is odd, draw an unbroken line (-). In the end, you will end up with two sets of three lines. Then, find each of your sets in the book and see what they mean!

Everyone's Favorite Treat: Ice Cream

Imagine our world without ice cream. It's something we don't want to do. Luckily, we don't need to because ice cream was invented in China around 200 BCE. It happened by accident when a mixture of rice and milk was frozen in the snow. Years later, the famous explorer, Marco Polo, saw ice cream while traveling to China. He went back to Italy and told them of the wonderful frozen treat.

Calligraphy

The most important ancient Chinese art form is calligraphy. It was first seen during the Han Dynasty in 206 BCE. People used animal hair - or sometimes a feather - to make brushes that were very flexible. They were then tied to a bamboo handle to make a brush. Writers used soot and animal glue to create a dried cake of ink.

People first painted on wood and bamboo. Later (from around 300 BCE), they started painting on silk. After paper was invented around AD 105, people used it for calligraphy, too. Have you ever tried calligraphy?

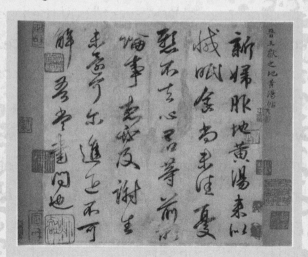

Chinese calligraphy
https://commons.wikimedia.org/wiki/File:Wang_Xianzi_Imitation_by_Tang_Dynasty.JPG

The Suspension Bridge

The Han Dynasty developed the suspension bridge, a flat roadway that is suspended from cables. By AD 90, Han engineers were building simple versions of these structures with wooden planks. Suspension bridges are still used today, and although the materials are improved, the method that the Ancient Chinese used, remains.

Tea

Tea has been very important in China, and it still is today. In fact, legend would suggest that tea had something to do with the story of silk. It is said that silk was discovered when a cocoon fell into a cup of imperial tea from a mulberry bush above.

The discovery of tea itself dates back to 2737 BCE when leaves from an overhanging Camellia bush fell into a cup of water. Emperor Shen Nung drank the tea, and so, the love of tea began.

Lacquer

You might be asking what lacquer is and why it is important. Well, lacquer is a liquid that you can use to protect your wooden furniture and make it shiny. You paint the liquid on wooden surfaces and then you wait for it to dry. If you apply it correctly, it can help your wooden furniture last much longer. It is also repels insects and water, so you can use it on a boat or even an umbrella. Now, that is awesome. Lacquer was first made in the Shang Dynasty.

Ancient China really has improved our lives greatly. Here is what they did for us:

A - Amazing tools to use everyday

N - New ways to use paper

C - Calligraphy and other beautiful ways to write on paper

I - Ice cream, yes, please!

E - Exciting ways to fish with the fishing rod and reel

N - Nice entertainment with kites

T - The wheelbarrow

C - Casting of iron

H - Handy matches to make fire

I - Interesting ways to do math with an Abacus

N - Neat ways to see the world by using hot air balloons

A - A great way to keep dry by using an umbrella

Warfare

Before the warring states of China were united, each state had its own territory and military. After the states became united, an organized army was formed. Although the states were united, emperors still wanted to claim more territory. An army was needed to conquer the surrounding land. For many centuries, China was often attacked by Mongol tribes to the north. China's military had to make sure that Chinese lands were safe! The soldiers worked very hard, and they had a stressful life. If something went wrong, it was their fault. They always had to give their best.

The Army

China was often at war during the Han Dynasty. There were also a lot of attacks from enemies north of the Han Dynasty. China's army was made up of men who served in the military for two years. If it was a peaceful time, the army was sent on missions to get more land for China. That meant that even in peaceful times, there was no rest for soldiers. There was always more land to find and seize.

Soldiers

During the Han Dynasty, all healthy men between the age of 23 and 56 had to serve in the army for two years. If there was an emergency, these men were called back to help even if their two years were over. If it was a peaceful time, the men who were still busy in their two years became guards. They had to stand at different points along the walls of cities and keep them safe.

Soldiers were not paid with money for their help; instead, they were paid with food. They had to wear their full uniform at all times. How hard would you work for a meal? These soldiers had no choice other than to work hard!

Weapons

The early armies in China used chariots and bronze weapons to fight. In the later years, as they got better at making weapons, they used iron weapons, too. The weapons were bows, arrows, and swords. Later they developed the crossbow, and people stopped using chariots. Crossbows were very helpful in battle. They could break the enemy's armor and travel 200 meters! So, it became one of the most important weapon in Ancient China. Crossbows became so useful that they were included in the burial tomb of Emperor Qin.

Ancient Chinese weapons Credit: Gary Todd
https://commons.wikimedia.org/wiki/File:Eighteen_Weapons_of_Ancient_China_(9883592815).jpg

Armor

Leather and metal were mostly used to make armor. To create strong armor, metal and leather pieces were stitched ver each other and then stitched to cloth. Soldiers could still move around and be protected. The Han Dynasty ntroduced helmets as part of armor. Helmets improved the chances of oldiers surviving battles.

o

i

s

Han iron scale armor replica
https://www.flickr.com/photos/1015613
34@N08/9873767864

Defense

Enemy tribes often attacked China, and the army had to defend their land. Some of the tribes trained their soldiers from a very young age, teaching them to fight and ride horses very well. Still, the army had a lot of soldiers who didn't fight well; they were just doing their two years of service.

49

Many of these attacks were hard, and China lost a lot of soldiers. It isn't really fair to let someone who just joined the army fight against someone who has been fighting since he was a small boy. But that was life in Ancient China.

Sun Tze and The Art of War

Sun Tzu statue Credit: 663highland
https://commons.wikimedia.org/wiki/
File:Enchoen27n3200.jpg

A famous Chinese general, Sun Tzu, wrote a very important book called <u>The Art of War</u>, and it was written 2,400 years ago! The book has 13 chapters, and it taught readers step-by-step ideas of how to win a war.

Sun Tzu means Master Sun, and he lived during the Spring and Autumn Period - from about 771 to 476 BCE. His family members were in the army, so he learned a lot about the battle as a boy. When he was a young man, he became an advisor to the warlord of the state of Wu, helping the warlord defeat his enemies. It is said that he wrote <u>The Art of War</u> on bamboo strips! Isn't it amazing how much writing has changed since then? Imagine reading your science textbook on bamboo?

The Heavenly horses

There were many different kinds of horses in Ancient China. The horses in South China were small and light. The horses in North China were big and strong.

The Heavenly Horses of Ancient China were very different. The horses were tall with a small head and a long neck. They had a long back with narrow bodies. Their legs were long. Their mane was thin. The thing that stood out about these horses was their sweat; it looked red, making people think of blood. This made them very popular in battle, because the red sweat scared the enemy.

The Terracotta Army

The first emperor of China, Emperor Qin Shi Huang, had a huge tomb for his burial. This was the Terracotta Army and there were more than 8,000 life size statues of soldiers buried with the emperor. The reason for this very full tomb was that Emperor Qin wanted to live forever. He always tried to find the true answer for living forever, the real "elixir of life". Eternal life wasn't the only thing he spent time and resources on. He also spent a lot of resources and time on building his own tomb. It was the largest single tomb that any leader in the world has ever had! Why did he want to share his final resting place with more than 8,000 terracotta soldiers?

He thought a massive army would keep him safe and help him be powerful in the afterlife. He died more than 2000 years ago in 210 BCE. We can still see the terracotta army today.

What do the soldiers look like?

The soldiers are life-size statues, and they are around 5 feet 11 inches tall. Some soldiers were as tall as b 6 foot 7 inches! Even though there as literally thousands of them, no two are alike. Isn't that amazing?

The soldiers are all of different ages. They have different hairstyles, and faces. They even have different facial expressions.

Some of them are angry, some are calm, and some seem ready for battle.

They also have different clothing and armor, but some have no armor at all. It is thought that the soldiers without armor might have been spies. These soldiers still impress us today, but imagine how impressive they must have been 2000 years ago! They were painted to look even more realistic. They were also covered with a special finish, called a lacquer finish.

They held onto real weapons - crossbows, daggers, maces, spears, and swords - which were the most used at that time. Emperor Qin took his afterlife power so seriously that he used real weapons in his terracotta army instead of giving them to his soldiers. So, they had to make more weapons for actual battle.

Terracotta soldier
Credit: shankar s. https://www.flickr.com/photos/shankaronline/35557414921

How did they build so many soldiers?

Can you imagine how long and how many people it took to build an army of 8,000 life-size statues? It has been estimated by archeologists that over 700,000 craftsmen worked on the project for many years. The bodies of the soldiers were made in an assembly line. There were molds for making the legs, arms, torsos, and heads. These pieces were then put together and then custom features such as ears, mustaches, hair, and weapons were added at a later time.

There are ten different head shapes for the soldiers. These different head shapes represent people from different areas of China - even with different personalities. The heads were made from customized molds, and as the last step, they were attached to the bodies. It is incredible to see more than 8,000 statues - each with a unique look.

Other statues

Emperor Qin Shi Huang's tomb is most famous for its terracotta soldiers, but there were several other statues that would keep Emperor Qin company in the afterlife. These other statues included 150 life-size cavalry horses and 130 chariots with 520 horses. These statues were buried with the army. Other figures have been found in other areas of the tomb. They are thought to be government officials and entertainers.

Han cavalry
https://commons.wikimedia.org/wiki/File:Dahuting_Tomb_mural,_cavalry_and_chariots,_Eastern_Han_Dynasty.jpg

Farmers discovered the Terracotta Army while they were digging a well in 1974 - more than 2,000 years after the burial of Emperor Qin! The emperor's tomb was located about a mile from where his army was stationed.

The Great Wall of China

The Great Wall of China is an ancient wall - and probably China's most famous feature. Parts of the wall were started in the 7th century BCE, but not entirely completed until the early 1900s by the Qing dynasty. It is made of cement, rocks, bricks, and powdered dirt. It was meant to protect the north from enemy attacks. It is the longest structure ever built by humans.

How long is the Great Wall of China? It is 13,171 miles 13,171 miles long. It is 30 feet wide, and it is 50 feet high. Sections of the wall started before the Ming Dynasty were made with stone and dirt that had been compacted. Later, bricks were used. The wall is incredible, with 7,000 watch towers, block houses for soldiers, and beacons for sending smoke signals.

Lao Tzu

Lao Tzu, who is also called Laozi or Lao Tze, was the head figure of Taoism - a spiritual practice. Some people say Lao Tze was a record-keeper in the court during the Zhou Dynasty. Other people say that is not true, and that he is just a myth. Some legends tell us that Lao Tzu was born as an old man with long earlobes who lived to be 990 years old. What do you think?

Lao Tzu
https://commons.wikimedia.org/wiki/File:Lao_Tzu_-_Project_Gutenberg_eText_15250.jpg

The legend tells us that Lao Tze was tired of working in the court, so he left and rode on a water buffalo to the western border of the Chinese empire. He was dressed as a farmer, but the guard at the border recognized him and asked him to write down his wisdom. Lao Tze wrote words that were so incredible that they became a sacred text called the <u>Tao Te Ching</u>. It is said that he was never seen again. Stories about Lao Tzu have been passed down through different Chinese philosophical schools for over two thousand years.

Today, at least twenty million Taoists live around the world, especially in China and Taiwan. They practice meditation, chant sacred texts, and worship various gods and goddesses in temples run by priests. Taoists also make pilgrimages to five sacred mountains in Eastern China to pray at the temples and absorb spiritual energy from these holy places, which are believed to be cared for by immortals.

Taoist temple

Confucius
https://commons.wikimedia.org/wiki/File:Confucius_statue_in_beijing_(cropped).jpg

Confucius, whose Chinese name was Kong Fu Zi, was born in 551 BCE in the Zhou Dynasty, on east coast of China. He was born to a "shi" class family.

The shi were middle-class people - not rich, not poor. They were not noble people, but they had more money than the common people.

He traveled between different states and advised governors who were at war. He believed people should be given opportunities - or chances to get more powerful or wealthy - based on their talents and not on what family they were born into.

He started his life as a shepherd before working in the government of his small town. He eventually became a top advisor to the local authorities.

Confucius proved his idea of being rewarded due to your talents (not your family) worked because he worked hard to create his own life.

Confucius spent his time learning and traveling. People started to notice him, and they wanted him to teach their sons. So, Confucius became the first private teacher in China. Before he was the first teacher, sons were taught by their families.

After a lot of studying and learning from different people, Confucius wrote a set of ideas called Confucianis. This was not a religion, but a way of life. It is a philosophy that can help people be their best; a set of rules that help people care more for others and be more responsible.

Confucianism's main ideas are:

- Always respect your elders
- Always be polite and gracious to other people
- It is important to learn, always
- Be a person with good morals
- Be kind, honest and loyal Be loyal, honest and kind
- Don't overdo things

It was only after his death that Confucianism became popular.

Buddhism

There are many forms of Buddhism around the world with Chinese Buddhism being one of the oldest forms. Chinese Buddhists believe in a combination of Taoism and Mahayana Buddhism. Yes, big words! Taoism is based on being humble and doing your religious duty. Mahayana Buddhism is more concerned with doing good for others, and everyone becoming "enlightened."

The Laughing Buddha is the most famous picture of the Buddha in China. Chinese Buddhism is different from original Buddhism because, in Chinese Buddhism, Buddha isn't just a teacher; he is a god, and his people should pray for his help.

Chinese Buddhists believe in a mix of Taoism and Buddhism. They pray to Buddha and Taoist gods. But, like Taoists, Chinese Buddhists also pray to their ancestors, thinking they need and want their help.

Chinese Buddhism is different in another way: how they picture Buddha. In the original Buddhist teachings, Buddha is very thin because he was always fasting (going without food). However, in Chinese Buddhism, the Laughing Buddha (or Budai) is shown as being fat and laughing. This is because the main goal of Chinese Buddhists is to be happy.

Dragon Boat Festival

A colorful festival was started during the Zhou Dynasty: The Dragon Boat Festival. Every year on the fifth day of the fifth lunar month of the Chinese calendar, the Dragon Boat Festival is celebrated.

The festival serves as a reminder of an Ancient Chinese poet, Qu Yuan, who jumped into a river and died; many believe he did it on purpose.

During the Dragon Boat Festival, traditions are eating rice dumplings, wearing perfume to protect people from evil beings, and exciting, colorful dragon boat racing. People enjoy making their own rice dumplings. They use banana leaves to cover a triangle-shaped rice ball with meat in the middle. Small sachets that smell sweet are given as presents.

Night of Sevens Festival

The Night of Sevens Festival was first celebrated during the Han Dynasty. It takes place on the seventh day of the seventh lunar month. It marks the love between two people.

A couple finds each other again after the Queen of Heaven separated them. One of the traditions during the festival is praying for a good husband. People also pray to the stars during the Night of the Sevens Festival.

Moon Festival

The Moon Festival is also known as the Mid-Autumn Festival. It started during the Zhou Dynasty, and happens in September. It is a celebration of the harvest.

Traditions during the festival are eating moon cakes - something that began under the Yuan Dynasty. Moon cakes are small round cakes, usually made with a buttery pastry and stuffed with a soft filling. They can be pressed into special molds to have  pretty shapes, or stamped with a special message.

Have you ever had a moon cake? There are moon cakes and sun cakes available today. Moon cakes are the more traditional cakes with one filling on the nside. Sun cakes are baked with an egg yolk in the middle of

Mid-Autumn Festival
Credit: Shizhao https://commons.wikimedia.org/wiki/File:Mid-Autumn_Festival-beijing.jpg

i

the cake, so when you bite into it, it looks like you are staring into the sun. Yum! Moon Festival is celebrated by having a big barbeque outside. Everyone celebrates happily as they eat together.

Double Ninth Festival

The number nine was very lucky in Ancient China. It was a good number for dragons and emperors. Therefore, on the ninth day of the ninth lunar month (usually in October), the Double Ninth Festival is celebrated.

Traditions on this day are drinking chrysanthemum tea. The tea is supposed to protect people from evil spirits. People also climb a hill or mountain.

Winter Solstice Festival

The shortest day of the year is celebrated with the Winter Solstice Festival. This celebration started during the Han Dynasty.

Traditions on this day are sacrificing to the ancestors. People have no work on the day; instead they can enjoy their day with family and friends.

Chinese New Year

This celebration is just as important today as it was in Ancient China. It is also celebrated the same way. In Ancient China, people would welcome the beginning of the New Year by setting off firecrackers. Back then, the firecrackers were made with gunpowder and bamboo.

Traditions of the celebration are making dishes with pork, chicken, and lamb. It is meant to make the land fertile for the year ahead. In Ancient China, people would hang sheep and chicken skins outside their homes, and burn incense. Today a very important part of the celebration is giving and receiving red envelopes. These envelopes contain money, and they are given to and by family members on New Year's Eve. People have a big New Year's Eve meal and then they play Mahjong (a popular Chinese game played with tiles) for hours. People like to give small oranges as gifts to family and friends because they are meant to bring good luck.

Chinese New Year festive costume
Credit: Dom Crossley https://www.flickr.com/photos/flashcurd/8499214042

The Lantern Festival

Red Lanterns
https://commons.wikimedia.org/wiki/File:Red_lanterns_in_Taichung_Park.jpg

The Lantern Festival was another important festival and is celebrated as a part of the New Year's celebration. The festival celebrates the full moon's light. It is celebrated on the 15th day of the first lunar month (between December and January).

Traditions of the festival include people holding feasts, dancing, and playing games near ponds, streams, and lakes. Sometimes people would float large lanterns on the water.

Richer people celebrated with more likable lamps. However, the emperor had an enormous light. So everyone spent all the money and material to make sure they will have a lucky year ahead.

The Chinese calendar has been used for thousands of years. It is still used today to mark traditional Chinese holidays.

The Chinese calendar was made by many of the Chinese dynasties of Ancient China.

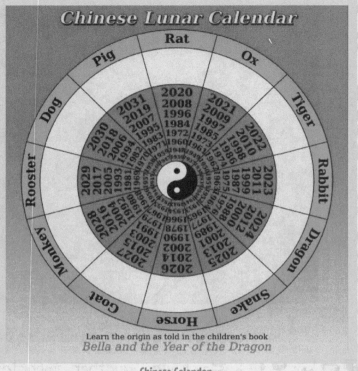

Learn the origin as told in the children's book
Bella and the Year of the Dragon

Chinese Calendar
https://freesvg.org/chinese-lunar-calendar-1

However, in 104 BCE, during Emperor Wu's rule of the Han Dynasty, the calendar we use today was created. This calendar is included the days, weeks, and months of a particular year, and was called the Tai Chu calendar.

Every year in the Chinese calendar is named after an animal. Twelve animals repeat in a cycle, so, every twelve years, the cycle repeats itself. It was believed that people had the same personalities as the animal of their birth year.

Let's look at the animals and what they mean.

Year of the Rat

Years: 1960, 1972, 1984, 1996, 2008, 2020

Personality of the rat: charming, loyal, and funny

Who do people who were born in the year of the rat get along with? They get along with people who were born in the year of the dragon and monkey. They do not get along with people who were born in the year of the horse.

Year of the Ox

Years: 1961, 1973, 1985, 1997, 2009, 2021

Personality of the ox: hardworking, serious, patient, and trustworthy

Who do people who were born in the year of the ox get along with? They get along with people who were born in the year of the snake and rooster. They do not get along with people who were born in the year of the sheep.

Year of the Tiger

Years: 1962, 1974, 1986, 1998, 2010

Personality of the tiger: aggressive, brave, ambitious, and intense

Who do people who were born in the year of the tiger get along with? They get along with people who were born in the year of the dog and horse. They do not get along with people who were born in the year of the monkey.

Year of the Rabbit

Years: 1963, 1975, 1987, 1999, 2011

Personality of the rabbit: popular, lucky, kind, and sensitive

Who do people who were born in the year of the rabbit get along with? They get along with people who were born in the year of the pig and sheep. They do not get along with people who were born in the year of the rooster.

Year of the Dragon

Years: 1964, 1976, 1988, 2000, 2012

Personality of the dragon: energetic, healthy and are lucky with the gift of good fortune and good luck

Who do people who were born in the year of the dragon get along with? They get along with people who were born in the year of the monkey and rat. They do not get along with people who were born in the year of the dog.

Year of the Snake

Years: 1965, 1977, 1989, 2001, 2013

Personality of the snake: smart, jealous, and generous

Who do people who were born in the year of the snake get along with? They get along with people who were born in the year of the rooster and ox. They do not get along with people who were born in the year of the pig.

Year of the Horse

Years: 1966, 1978, 1990, 2002

Personality of the horse: like to travel, attractive, impatient, and popular

Who do people who were born in the year of the horse get along with? They get along with people who were born in the year of the tiger and dog. They do not get along with people who were born in the year of the rat.

Year of the Sheep

Years: 1967, 1979, 1991, 2003

Personality of the sheep or goat: creative, shy, and unsure

Who do people who were born in the year of the sheep get along with? They get along with people who were born in the year of the rabbit and pig. They do not get along with people who were born in the year of the ox.

Year of the Monkey

Years: 1968, 1980, 1992, 2004

Personality of the monkey: curious, naughty, and clever

Who do people who were born in the year of the monkey get along with? They get along with people who were born in the year of the dragon and rat. They do not get along with people who were born in the year of the tiger.

Year of the Rooster

Years: 1969, 1981, 1993, 2005

Personality of the rooster: honest, neat, practical, and proud

Who do people who were born in the year of the rooster get along with? They get along with people who were born in the year of the snake and ox. They do not get along with people who were born in the year of the rabbit.

Year of the Dog

Years: 1958, 1970, 1982, 1994, 2006

Personality of the dog: loyal, honest, sensitive, and moody

Who do people who were born in the year of the dog get along with? They get along with people who were born in the year of the tiger and horse. They do not get along with people who were born in the year of the dragon.

Year of the Pig

Years: 1959, 1971, 1983, 1995, 2007

Personality of the pig: intelligent, sincere, perfectionistic, and noble

Who do people who were born in the year of the pig get along with? They get along with people who were born in the year of the rabbit and sheep. They do not get along with people who were born in the year of the pig.

Could you find your birth year? Do you share the personality traits of your birth year animal?

Years ago, the Jade emperor wanted to measure time for his birthday. He told all the animals that if they could swim across the river, there would be a month of the zodiac calendar named after them.

All the animals ined up excitedly. It was only Rat and Cat that were nervous because they are not good swimmers. They asked Ox if they could sit on his back while he swam; he said it would be ok.

The race started and Rat and Cat sat on Ox's back while he swam. Ox was a strong swimmer, so Rat and Cat were happy. However, when they got close to the end of the race, Rat pushed Cat into the water. Then Rat jumped off of Ox's head and won the race.

Rat had tricked Ox. Ox came second and would forever be after Rat in the Zodiac calendar.

The Jade emperor saw that Rat won and he celebrated. "Well done, Rat," he said, "You are first on the Chinese Zodiac calendar."

What a sneaky and smart Rat!

Part 2:
Ancient Japan for Kids

ANCIENT JAPAN
FOR KIDS

A CAPTIVATING GUIDE TO ANCIENT JAPANESE HISTORY
FROM PREHISTORY TO THE HEIAN PERIOD

CAPTIVATING HISTORY

INTRODUCTION

Have you ever wondered what Japan was like long ago? The Japanese people have had a long and interesting history, filled with warrior queens, emperors, and discoveries that have changed the world. Both parents and children will enjoy learning about Ancient Japan in this fun, up-to-date history of the Japanese people.

The Japanese people have always been innovative. For example, did you know that the Japanese were the first people to create pottery? That might not sound important, but there were no plates, bowls, jars, or pots before they invented pottery. The ancient people in Japan invented all of that.

In this book, you'll get an up-close view of Ancient Japan. You'll learn about the warring clans that roamed the islands, about the emperors who united them, and the myths they told. This book has all the relevant and up-to-date information that you need to explore Ancient Japanese history. Get ready to dive in and learn how the Japanese people have thrived on their islands and changed the world.

Chapter 1: The Jōmon Period

The Jōmon period is the first part of Japanese history, and it lasted from about 13,000 BCE to 300 BCE. That's a really long time - over 12,000 years - and the Jōmon people lived all over the islands that form modern Japan off the Eastern coast of Asia.

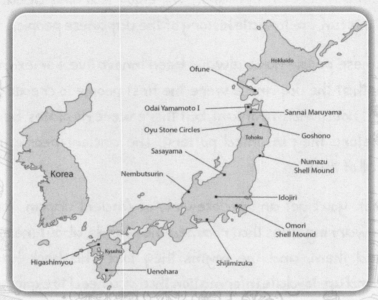

Jōmon Period Map

But were there people on the islands before the Jōmon period began?

Most archeologists say yes. They have found evidence of human activity, such as bones and really old stone tools, from as early as 500,000 BCE. By working with archeologists, historians used these discoveries to learn that these first people were nomadic hunters and gatherers, which means they moved around to hunt and find food. The first people in Japan probably crossed on land bridges during the last Ice Age and followed giant elk and Naumann elephants, but historians don't really know because nobody could write yet. It probably seems strange, but there was a time long ago that no one could write. Because of this, there are no books, papers, or diaries from the people living in ancient Japan at this time. Without these written stories, historians have to work with archeologists to find clues and discover what really happened long ago.

The Jōmon period started in 13,000 BCE with the invention of pottery. Why was pottery such a big deal to the ancient people of Japan? Unlike us today, they didn't have plates, bowls, and pots that they could buy at the store. In fact, before pottery was invented, they didn't have it at all. By inventing pottery, the Jōmon people invented a better way to cook and store food, which helped them live better lives. When they first started making pottery, all their pots looked similar. As they practiced, though, they began to make pots that had specific jobs and specific shapes. The more interesting shapes come from later in the Jōmon period, after the people had been able to practice making pottery for hundreds of years.

Jomon Period Pottery (https://flic.kr/p/FALbtf)

Just like us, the Jōmon people decorated the things they had. To make their pottery pretty, they would press cords and ropes into the wet clay to make patterns. If you have some patience and creativity, you can make almost an endless variety of patterns. Historians separate the Jōmon period into six periods based on the common pottery decorations and the advancements of village life.

Here are the six historical periods that make up the whole Jōmon period:

Incipient Jōmon (10,000 - 7,500 BCE)

Initial Jōmon (7,500 - 4,000 BCE)

Early Jōmon (4,000 - 3,000 BCE)

Middle Jōmon (3,000 - 2,000 BCE)

Late Jōmon (2,000 - 1,000 BCE)

Final Jōmon (1000 - 300 BC)

Did you know that "jōmon" can be translated into English as "cord-marked"? The name came from Edward S. Morse. In 1877, Morse was teaching zoology (the study of animals) to students at Tokyo University. One day, he was riding a Japanese train, and he noticed some broken pieces of pottery on the ground outside the window. No one had ever noticed them before, and he was curious about them. When Morse went to investigate, he discovered the first evidence of the Jōmon people. That's how the Jōmon period got its name.

Now, people don't tend to use pottery in hunting and gathering communities because it breaks easily. Pottery is more likely to be used in permanent villages. So, the pottery shows historians that the Jōmon people began to settle into permanent houses and villages. Permanent houses are better for using pottery, and historians believe that the Jōmon people were among the first to build permanent houses and villages. The Jōmon houses were either above-ground homes or pit dwellings and were about the size of one bedroom today. Four or five people lived in each one. Can you imagine having to share your room with four more people? Space was tight in Jōmon houses!

Reconstructed Jomon period houses (https://flic.kr/p/2hS1Hfp)

Reconstructed Jomon period houses (https://flic.kr/p/2hRYcHj)

Even though the houses were small, people started living in villages because they worked together to farm. While they did still hunt and fish, the Jōmon people learned how to grow food using tools made from stone, wood, and bone. Some of their favorites were chestnuts, beans, gourds, and gobō (also called burdock root). They would then boil or store the food in their pots and other containers. The Jōmon people had more food than ever before thanks to farming and pottery.

Jomon man and woman reproduction (https://flic.kr/p/2hS2Jiv)

With so much food, villages continued to grow, and some people lived to be over 65 years old. While you might think many of these villages were small, historians have found a village that once had 500 people living there. For that time, that was a lot of people! The village is called the Sannai Maruyama site, and it's located in Northern Japan. The village was so big that archeologists found a watch tower and a large building where the community worked on projects together. Archeologists have also found proof that the Jōmon people traded with other villages.

Some of the things they received were jade, amber, obsidian, and asphalt. They needed the asphalt to make arrows so they could continue hunting, and they used some of the minerals and stones to make jewelry. Now that they didn't have to worry about being hungry, they could focus on making and trading pretty things.

Of course, historians are learning more about the Jōmon people every year. They are still investigating the clues these people left behind, but they do know the Jōmon people invented pottery and worked together in villages to farm. This seems to have been a peaceful period, but historians are always looking for more clues to tell them how the Jōmon people lived their lives.

Chapter 1: Challenge

Can you fill in the blank for each of these sentences with one of the words below?

Pottery   Edward S. Moore   Rope
Farming villages   Nomadic hunters and gatherer
Sannai Maruyama site

1. The first people in Japan were _____.

2. The Jōmon people invented _____.

3. They decorated their pottery by pressing _____ into the wet clay.

4. _____ first discovered Jōmon pottery in 1877.

5. The Jōmon people lived in _____ and grew chestnuts, beans, gourds, and gobō.

6. The largest village archeologists have found is the _____ in Northern Japan.

Chapter 2: The Yayoi Period

The second period of Ancient Japanese history is called the Yayoi period. It lasted from 300 BCE to 300 CE, which is 600 years.

The Yayoi people were different from the Jōmon people, but where did the Yayoi people come from? Everyone comes from somewhere, and historians believe the Yayoi people migrated from China and Korea into Japan.

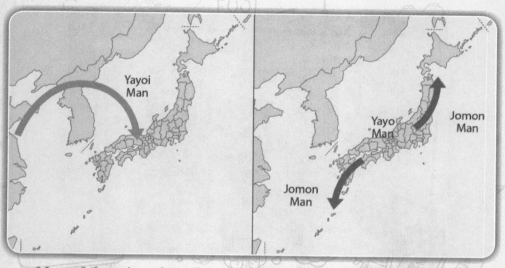

Map of the migration of the Yayoi people and the Jomon people

When the Yayoi people moved in, they brought their culture with them. The Yayoi people had a very different way of life, but they may have kept some parts of the Jōmon culture. They were focused on rice farming and introduced rice to the islands of Japan. To grow rice, the people moved into lowlands with lots of water, where rice paddies were easier to grow. They settled together into permanent farming villages to make farming easier, just like the Jōmon people did. Can you imagine having to run a whole farm by yourself? It would be a lot of work to do by yourself! To make farming easier, the Yayoi people worked together to farm rice. They used special shoes to make it easier. The shoes were wide and flat, which prevented the people from sinking into the rice paddies. It was a lot like when you go to the pool and use a kickboard or other floaties to help you swim. These shoes were called platformed tageta sandals. The Yayoi people also learned how to make metal tools such as hoes and axes, which are better for farming than stone tools.

Yayoi people clothing
(https://commons.wikimedia.org/wiki/File:Yayoi_people_attires.JPG)

Once they learned how to work with metal, the Yayoi people started making all kinds of metal objects. Now that they had plenty of food, they could focus on other things, like art. People tend to do this across civilizations and across time; it even still affects people today. The Yayoi people mostly used bronze and copper, and they made mirrors, swords, and ceremonial bells called dōtaku. A version of these bells is still still used today in some temples in Japan!

Dōtaku Bronze Bells (https://flic.kr/p/G7aVRJ)

Historians think the Yayoi used their metal art to worship nature gods and pray for good harvests. They seemed to have celebrated festivals to thank the nature gods for a good harvest and to ask for a good harvest next year. However, historians don't know all the details of these religious festivals. The Yayoi people didn't leave behind any writing for us, so historians have to put the clues together from what they left behind. Historians have to do this a lot, especially with ancient civilizations,

The Yayoi people also made swords and other weapons like arrows. They made armor and shields out of strong wood. The bronze swords were used for religious ceremonies, but the iron swords were used for war.

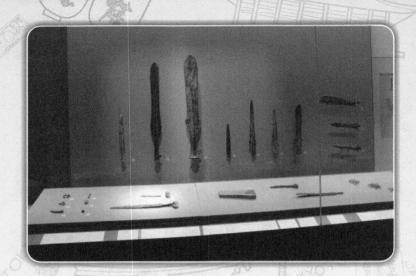

Yayoi Period Bronze Weapons (https://flic.kr/p/FAPHrw)

The Jōmon people don't seem to have fought wars, but the Yayoi people definitely did. The villages began to fight with each other over farmland, water, and food. All these things were important to growing rice in the rice paddies. Without them, people would starve. Because farming can be unpredictable at times, the growing population of ancient Japan would go to war over food. So, the strong villages began to take over the weaker villages.

By around 100 CE, there were about 100 clans in Japan. People began to take strong leadership positions in their villages to defend themselves from others, which started the ruling class in Ancient Japan. Rulers have been a big part of Ancient Japanese history ever since the Yayoi period. They started to grow a political system, which focuses on building and keeping up with a government. Governments can be big or small, but they are supposed to keep the people they are ruling safe from invading armies. Another part of the job of a government is to collect taxes and make laws, which the 100 clans in Japan started to do. We know this because the Book of Han from the Chinese Han

Dynasty (which occurred during the Yayoi period in Japan) describes it. This book is important because this is the first time Japan is mentioned in writing in the history of the world. The Yayoi people didn't have a writing system yet; a lot of what historians know about the Yayoi period actually comes from Ancient Chinese historical records.

The Chinese historical records also mention Priestess Queen Himiko. She ruled the Yamatai kingdom around 220 CE. Queen Himiko united 30 different clans into her kingdom through war and conquest, and then she brought peace to southern Japan. After bringing peace, Queen Himiko turned her kingdom's focus to trade. They traded with the countries and villages around them to get resources they needed, like metal. Trading was very common because no one in Japan had invented money yet. In return, the Yayoi people traded jewelry and other precious resources with other cities that were far away.

Can you imagine having to travel for days to trade for what you needed?

The Yayoi people couldn't just go to the store down the street and buy what they needed every week. They had to travel to trading centers. Because trade was important to the Yayoi people, the trading centers quickly became the biggest cities because everyone wanted to be able to get everything they needed after such a long trip. The biggest trading center was called Asahi, and it was located in Southern Japan. After

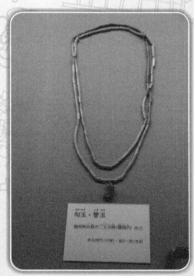

Yayoi people jewelry
(https://flic.kr/p/GquNSi)

Queen Himiko died in 248 CE, Queen Iyo took over the Yamatai kingdom, but historians don't know much about her yet.

The Yayoi period is important to Ancient Japanese history. These people introduced rice and metal to the islands. They settled into villages, developed governments, and fought the first wars of Japan. They are even the ancestors of modern Japanese people! The Yayoi have influenced a lot of modern Japanese culture, and they made an impact on Japan that is hard to forget.

Chapter 2: Challenge

Can you match the word or person with the correct description?

a. Yayoi period

b. Queen Himiko

c. Book of Han

d. Dōtaku

e. Rice paddies

a. The history book from the Chinese Han dynasty that first mentions Japan.

b. The wet lowlands where the Yayoi people grew rice.

c. The second period of Ancient Japanese history.

d. Ceremonial bells made of bronze and copper.

e. The priestess queen of the Yamatai kingdom around 220 CE.

Chapter 3: The Kofun Period

The Kofun Period is the third period of Ancient Japanese history, and it lasted from 300 CE to 538 CE. That's only 238 years, but the Kofun Period still experienced many changes in Japanese culture. It was during the Kofun Period that the Japanese people began to experience a more unified country.

Did you know that the word "kofun" can be translated into English as "old tomb"? The distinctive tombs that were popular during this time are where the Kofun Period gets its name. Different cultures have different ways of honoring their dead. The way we have funerals today is different from how the Kofun people had funerals. Instead of digging graves for their dead loved ones, the Kofun people constructed burial mounds out of rocks or naturally forming hills. They usually shaped the natural hills into the final shape of a burial mound, which meant they were carving the ground like an artist. It would have been really hard to do. The burial mounds were usually up on the high ground that overlooked villages and rice paddies. Everyone could see the burial mounds, and they probably impressed any visitors to the Japanese islands. Do you think these burial mounds are impressive?

The Ishibutai Kofun in Asuka
(https://commons.wikimedia.org/wiki/File:Ishibutai_Kofun,_sekishitsu.jpg)

The burial mounds came in several different shapes. The most common shapes were circles, squares, and keyhole shapes. While the shapes were all similar, the size of each burial mound could vary widely. The smallest ones are only about 10 feet long, but the biggest ones are over 1,200 feet long! That's as long as four football fields! Each burial mound was intended for only one person - and commoners had smaller burial mounds. You had to be an important member of the ruling class, like an emperor, to get a large burial mound.

The burial mounds popular during the Kofun period are all over the Japanese islands, but there are many of them in Central Japan. If you travel to Japan, you can still see them today.

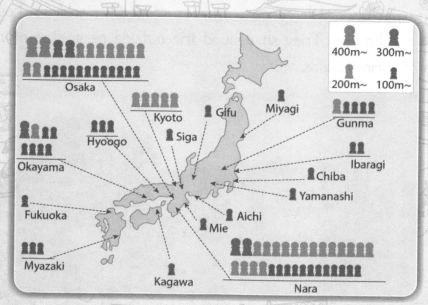

Distribution Map of Kofun in Japan

The two biggest examples of the Kofun burial mounds are the Daisen Kofun and the Goshikizuka Kofun. The Daisen Kofun is so big that historians and archeologists think it must have taken four years and 1,000 workers to build it. Like all the burial mounds from this period,

91

the Daisen Kofun has large stone rooms inside the mound that are the burial rooms for the person who has died. It even has a moat around it like a castle! Some of the really big burial mounds had moats.

The Goshikizuka Kofun is another big burial mound in Japan. It has recently been restored by historians and archeologists, which means that they have repaired the burial mound and made it look like the original people had made it. Restoring historical sites is a big part of being a historian and archeologist. The job takes a lot of research, but it helps people like us to see history come alive right before our eyes!

The Goshikizuka Kofun now has its stone-paved paths and its outdoor monuments back in their right places. These outdoor statues are called haniwa, which are little ceramic statues shaped like soldiers, houses, boats, and horses. They sit around the outside perimeter of many different burial mounds.

Haniwa statues (https://flic.kr/p/LR8QiX)

Inside, the burial mounds are also decorated. Some of the tombs have wall paintings. Most of the people buried in the burial mounds were buried with treasures. We don't usually bury people with treasure now, but the people of the Kofun era did - especially if the tomb belonged to someone in the ruling class, that person would be buried with mirrors, armor, swords, farming equipment, jewelry, and horse-riding equipment. All this stuff was important to the Kofun people and their culture, so they made sure that their dead had everything they needed. As the Kofun period continued, burying royalty with armor and swords became very popular.

Historians think that these burial practices might be linked to the changes happening in Japan during the Kofun Period. At the beginning of the Kofun period, the Yamato clan began gaining power in Central Japan. Some historians think the Yamato clan is the same kingdom as the Yamatai kingdom, which Queen Himiko ruled during the Yayoi period. Unfortunately, historians don't know for sure if these two kingdoms are the same group. Writing didn't begin in Japan until late in the Kofun period, so there are no written Japanese documents from the beginning of the Yamato clan.

The Yamato clan worked on uniting Japan as one kingdom by bringing together all the smaller villages and states. They started by creating a loose group of local government leaders who all agreed to cooperate with each other. As the Yamato clan continued to conquer both southern and northern Japan, they created a hierarchy and assigned special jobs to different government leaders. At the top of the hierarchy was the Great King. He was called the Okimi, and he was the strongest leader of the Yamato clan. Eventually, the position of the okimi, or great king, changed into the position of emperor. The rulers of the Yamato clan made the throne hereditary, which means that it passed from parent to child. In most ancient civilizations, the father would pass the throne to his oldest son. Did you know that the current rulers of Japan are directly related to the first great kings of the Yamato clan? The reign of this family has lasted all this time, passed through hereditary, and that makes the Yamato Dynasty the world's longest dynasty.

As the Yamato kingdom continued to grow in power during the Kofun period, they started to reach out to other kingdoms in China and Korea, including the kingdom of Baekje in Korea.

They wanted to find sources of iron, which they needed to make weapons and farming tools. They also wanted to make alliances with other kingdoms. Alliances are promises kingdoms make to support each other in war against other kingdoms and also to not start a war with each other. Powerful kingdoms need alliances. As part of the Yamato kingdom's alliances, they saw and adopted the Chinese writing style. For the first time, the Japanese people began to write things down, and the Nihon Shoki is Japan's history book from the Kofun period, but it also contains myths and legends.

While the people during the Kofun period learned how to write, they also experienced other changes. One of the big changes that helped the commoners was the Kamado stove from China. Before this, everyone had cooked their food over open fire pits. While that may be fun when we go camping, cooking over a fire pit can be hard every day. Can you imagine how hard that would be? Although the commoners still lived in small, ground-level huts, they at least had the Kamado stove to make cooking a little easier.

Kofun Era House
(https://commons.wikimedia.org/wiki/File:Kofun_Era_House_(29434898824).jpg)

Religion was also a big part of people's lives, as they worshiped the nature gods and prayed for good harvests. They also worshiped the spirits of clan ancestors at shrines. They believed that this worship would give them good harvests and help them live good lives. Then, in 538 CE, the kingdom of Baekje in Korea sent a Buddhist statue to Emperor Kinmei.

Buddhism Statues
(https://commons.wikimedia.org/wiki/File:Bronze_Buddhism_Statue_(29949526762).jpg)

Starting a new religion was scary for Emperor Kinmei, so he asked his advisors what he should do. His top two advisors had different opinions. Soga No Iname wanted to adopt Buddhism immediately, but Mononobe No Okoshi said that the new religion would anger the gods the Japanese already worshiped. The emperor allowed Soga No Iname to take the statue home while he decided what to do. Soga No Iname made his house into a Buddhist temple. Soon after that, a huge plague broke out over the Yamato kingdom. Many people got sick and died. Everyone was afraid, and Mononobe No Okoshi argued that the plague was a punishment from the island gods. Emperor Kinmei agreed, and they burnt Soga No Iname's house to the ground - trying to appease the nature gods.

Soga No Iname was angry that Mononobe No Okoshi burnt his house to the ground and threw the Buddhist statue into a nearby river. This started a fight between the two men and their clans that would not be resolved for many years. In fact, the introduction of the Buddhist statue and fighting that happened because of it is what started the Asuka period, which is the next period of Ancient Japanese history.

Chapter 3: Challenge

Can you fill in the blank for each of these sentences with one of the words below?

Yamato dynasty	Emperor Kinmei	Daisen Kofun
Haniwa	Nihon Shoki	Yamato clan	Kofun

1. The _____ is the world's longest dynasty.

2. _____ can be translated into English as 'old tomb.'

3. The little ceramic statues shaped like soldiers, houses, boats, and horses that sit outside of the burial mounds are called _____.

4. The _____ united Japan.

5. _____ received a Buddhist statue, which started a fight between his top two advisors.

6. Japan's history book about the Kofun period is called the _____.

7. The _____ is one of the biggest burial mounds. It took four years to build and even has a moat.

Chapter 4: The Asuka Period

The Asuka period is the fourth period of Ancient Japanese history, and it lasted from 538 CE to 710 CE. That's 172 years exactly, which is a really short period of time when talking about history. This period is still important because the Yamato kingdom changed a lot during these 172 years.

Map of Japan with Nara marked

Did you know that Asuka is one of the ancient cities of Japan? It was even the capital of Japan during the Asuka period, which is how historians named this part of Japanese history. The Yamato kingdom brought together much of its power during the Asuka period. This is the first time that they really established an emperor! Although clan leaders and kings had been ruling Japan before the Asuka period, it wasn't until now that the Japanese officially established an emperor.

The first emperor of Japan was Emperor Kinmei. You might remember him from the last chapter. He was given a Buddhist statue, and his advisors fought over it.

Emperor Kinmei is in both chapters because he was emperor during parts of both the Kofun Period and the Asuka Period. His reign overlaps the two periods: he started his reign in 531 AD and died in 571 AD. Emperor Kinmei is best remembered as the first historical emperor of Japan.

Weren't there kings and emperors before Emperor Kinmei? Yes, there were, but historians do not have written proof of them; all they have are legendary stories. Although stories are fun to tell, they aren't always completely true. Emperor Kinmei is the first emperor to have written proof, so he is the first historical emperor of Japan.

While he was ruling, Emperor Kinmei received a Buddhist statue, which caused fighting between the people who wanted to adopt Buddhism as a new religion and those who wanted to stick to the old religion. The old religion was called Shintō. It is still a religion in Japan today, and it focuses on ancestor worship and sacred objects like swords and mirrors. Buddhism is different. Buddhism is about peace and harmony with everything. It doesn't just include not fighting with your siblings. It also includes being respectful of nature and playing your part in the universe. There are many different gods in Buddhism, and they aren't the same as the Shintō gods.

People tend to be very protective of their religion, so there was much fighting when Buddhism was first introduced during Emperor Kinmei's reign. The fighting finally quieted down during the reign of Empress Suiko and Prince Shotoku, who was her regent. A regent is someone who rules the kingdom in place of the current rightful ruler. It usually happens because the rightful ruler is still a child. Empress Suiko and Prince Shotoku were the most important rulers of the Asuka Period, and they ruled Japan from 594 AD to 622 AD.

Prince Shotoku liked Buddhism and helped make it an important part of Japanese culture. He and Empress Suiko built Buddhist temples, some of which are still around today. They are made from wood, and they are beautiful.

Prince Shotoku Hall (https://flic.kr/p/aYAfjX)

Prince Shotoku also changed the government. Before he came to power, the government was suffering from a lot of corruption. People were trying to use the government to get things they wanted for themselves. They got their position by inheriting it from their fathers. To stop the corruption, Prince Shotoku made more of the positions based on your ability to do the job, not on who your parents were. That may seem obvious to us now. We know that the best person to do a job is the person who has trained for it and has the most knowledge. However, the ancient Japanese were more focused on heredity, or the passing down of family goods and titles to your children. So, Prince Shotoku made more positions based on ability, which reduced government corruption and focused the ruling power with the national government. The Japanese people liked both him and Empress Suiko, and they mourned the prince and the empress when they died.

Crown Prince Shotoku (574-622 with his two sons)
(https://commons.wikimedia.org/wiki/File:Prince_Shotoku.jpg#/media/File:Prince_Shotoku.jpg)

In 645 CE, the Fujiwara clan staged a coup against the Yamato government. A coup is when a group of people overthrows an existing government. It's usually a surprise - but not always a good one. The Fujiwara clan successfully overthrew the Soga clan, who had been running the Yamato government under the emperor. Fujiwara no Kamatari, who was the leader of the Fujiwara clan, took away most of the emperor's power and made some other changes to the government. Some things he changed were taxes, laws, and social classes. Can you imagine living during a time of so much change? It might be a little frightening, and it might also be overwhelming because everything you know would be changing. The Asuka period had a lot of this kind of change because people started fighting over who had the most power in the government.

Fujiwara-Kamatari
(https://commons.wikimedia.org/wiki/File:Fujiwara-Kamatari-LACMA.jpg#/media/File:Fujiwara-Kamatari-LACMA.jpg)

All this change and fighting led to the Jinshin Incident. When Emperor Tenji died in 671 CE, the Soga clan fought with the Fujiwara clan to control the government. The fighting only lasted until 672 CE, but it was intense. When Emperor Temmu finally took the throne in 672 CE, he remembered how bad the fighting had been. To stop anything like that from happening again, Emperor Temmu limited the number of people in the imperial family who could claim the throne. He said that only people who were direct descendants of himself and his wife Jito could possibly have a claim to the throne. Because he and his sons were supposed to marry only within the Fujiwara clan, the Soga clan could no longer claim the throne.

While all this fighting over the government was happening, Japan was also developing relationships with Korea and China. Just like you, countries need to make friends, and between countries, this friendship is called an alliance. Part of the reason that Prince Shotoku liked Buddhism so much was that China and Korea liked Buddhism. Having the same religion as other countries made Japan more popular. As Japan interacted with China and Korea, they began to share their cultures. The Japanese style of writing is like the Chinese style because Japan was given examples of Chinese literature. This influenced the Japanese government, and it even inspired the writing of the Seventeen Article Constitution in 604 CE.

Of course, Korea also influenced Japan, especially the Baekje kingdom of Korea. It was common for teachers and artists from the Baekje kingdom to travel in Japan. They first introduced Buddhism to Emperor Kinmei, and they also taught the Japanese how to build beautiful wooden buildings. All this sharing between China and Korea helped shape Japan and its culture during the Asuka period with all its fighting. Japan started to focus more on art once the fighting stopped, and that change led Japan into the next stage of Ancient Japanese history: the Nara period.

Chapter 4: Challenge

Can you match the word or person with the correct description?

1. Fujiwara no Kamatari

2. Jinshin Incident

3. Asuka

4. Emperor Kinmei

5. Prince Shotoku

6. Shintō

7. Buddhism

a. First historical emperor of Japan

b. Leader of the Fujiwara clan

c. The ancient religion of Japan focused on ancestor worship.

d. Regent for Empress Suiko

e. The capital of Japan during the Asuka period in Japanese history.

f. The fight between the Fujiwara clan and the Soga clan from 671-672 AD over who had the most power in the government.

g. Religion that focuses upon peace and harmony between everything.

Chapter 5: The Nara Period

The Nara period is the fifth period of Ancient Japanese history, and it lasted from 710 CE to 794 CE. That's only 84 years! Many historians see the Nara period as a transition between the Asuka period and the very important Heian period, but the Nara period is also special. Even though it is short and had many people fighting for power, the Nara period is best remembered for its art.

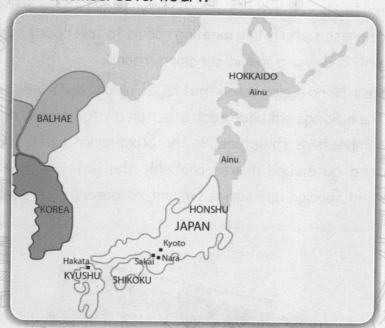

Map of Japan in 750 CE

Did you know that the capital of Japan has not always been in the same city? Throughout history, emperors moved the capital all over the island. During the Nara period, the capital of Japan was in Nara, which is a city in Japan that you can still visit today. You can think of Nara as the first true capital of Japan because it was built to be the permanent capital. Of course, that did not last. Emperors in later historical periods would move the capital yet again.

Nara was built to look like the Chinese capital of the Tang Dynasty. That city was called Chang'an. Empress Genmei ruled Japan during this point in history, and she made sure the city was organized like Chang'an, so the streets were planned and looked like a grid. There were two halves of the city, and the imperial palace split them. The empress lived in the imperial palace - a nice place to live - and not only did the empress have everything she needed to be comfortable, but she also had everything she needed to work. It was like working from home! There were offices for the empress's staff, two meeting rooms to talk about running the government, and even a special ceremony room.

The palace in Nara is also called the Heijo Palace, and it was beautiful. Each of the buildings sat near each other on a large compound. One of the most impressive structures is the Suzakumon Gate. It was the south-facing gate, and it was probably the gate from which the empress met foreign emissaries (important government people from

Heijo Palace

(https://commons.wikimedia.org/wiki/File:Heijo_Palace,_Suzaku-mon-2.jpg#/media/File:Heijo_Palace,_Suzaku-mon-2.jp

other countries). Although the original Nara palace is now gone, the modern Japanese government is rebuilding parts for visitors to see. They have rebuilt the Former Audience Hall, where the empress would have important meetings and ceremonies, and they are working to rebuild the Suzakumon Gate. You can visit the Nara palace today and imagine what it might have been like to be the emperor during the Nara period.

Because Nara was the capital city of Japan, many aristocrats, or people who had a high social class and worked in the government, moved to Nara when Empress Genmei moved. They built houses of their own, which meant other people had to move to Nara to support the city. Can you imagine a city that didn't have grocery stores or gas stations? It wouldn't be a good city. So, people moved in to help grow food, take care of the houses, teach at the new university, and organize the temples. With all these people moving to Nara, some historians think the city's population was as large as 200,000 people! That's a lot of people living and working together to make everything work right.

Empress Genmei didn't only make Nara into a great city. She and her successor Empress Gensho also made sure the first Japanese books were finished. These two books are called The Kojiki and the Nihon Shoki, which translates into English as "Chronicle of Japan." These books are Japan's earliest written histories. The Kojiki was finished first in 712 CE, and it tells a lot of the mythology of the Japanese people in the Japanese language. It also connects the imperial line of emperors all the way back to the Japanese gods themselves! While this probably wasn't completely true, they wrote it down because they wanted people to respect the emperor and obey the laws.

The Nihon Shoki was finished in 720 CE, and historians think this history book was intended for foreigners. It was written in Chinese, and it doesn't include as much mythology as The Kojiki does. Historians use both books to learn about Japanese history, but they have to be careful because there is so much mythology in these books too. We want our history to be as factually accurate as possible, so historians have to try to sort out the myth from the facts.

The Nara period didn't just have the first books in Japanese history. While the upper class was enjoying life, the lower class was having trouble. The peasantry survived by farming, and the Nara period had many droughts and famines. The droughts meant there wasn't enough water to grow the rice and other crops the Japanese people needed to survive, and the famines meant that there wasn't enough food for everyone to eat. To make things even worse, a smallpox pandemic happened. Many people got sick and died from the disease. Historians think Japan lost 25-35% of its people to smallpox. Can you imagine how the people might have felt back then? They didn't have science to explain how diseases spread or why droughts happen. If you didn't understand what was happening, it might be a little scary.

The Japanese people were very scared. Emperor Shomu wanted to help his people, but he didn't know how to do it. So, he declared that all these bad things were signs that the Japanese gods were angry with the people. Emperor Shomu blamed the droughts, famines, and pandemic on a lack of morality (or good living, following rules that line up with your beliefs). Morality is usually connected to religion. To help the people live with better morality, Emperor Shomu ordered the special construction of Buddhist temples all over the country.

Kofukuji Buddhist temple (https://flic.kr/p/2hBuMKf)

In Japan, the temples were built in every providence (like a state), usually close to the main cities. The Kofukuji Buddhist temple is one of the famous temples. It was in Yamashina, but it was taken down and rebuilt in Nara when Empress Genmei made Nara the capital. It was an important temple and even helped decide government policy sometimes.

Another famous Buddhist temple is the Diabutsuden, translated as "The Great Buddha Hall." It is home to the largest Buddha statue in the world, which is called the Great Buddha. The statue took almost ten years to finish, and it is 49 feet tall. It would take nine adults standing on top of each other to reach the top of the Great Buddha. It's really big! The Great Buddha still exists today, and you can visit the Diabutsuden in Japan to see it for yourself.

The Japanese people weren't only building Buddhist temples; they also continued to follow Shinto. The most famous Shinto shrine from the Nara period is the Kasuga-Taisha, and is in a forest near Nara. The legend around this shrine says that one of the Japanese gods appeared riding a deer right where the shrine now stands. To this day, deer are allowed to roam freely at the shrine, and many of the lanterns there are decorated with pictures of deer.

Kasuga-Taisha, a Shinto shrine, Nara Period
(https://commons.wikimedia.org/wiki/File:Kasuga-taisha,_chumon-1.jpg#/media/File:Kasuga-taisha,_chumon-1.jpg)

The Nara period ended in 794 CE when Emperor Kammu moved the capital of Japan to Heiankyo. The Japanese government had experienced a lot of fighting over power. Aristocrats wanted more power, and they were using plots and violence to get it. Emperor Kammu moved the capital to try to stop the fighting. This move ended the Nara period and started the Heian period, the last period of Ancient Japanese history.

Chapter 5: Challenge

Can you fill in the blank for each of these sentences with one of the words below?

> Suzakumon Gate   Buddhist temples   The Kojiki
> Nihon Shoki   Empress Genmei   Kasuga-Taisha

1. The south facing gate that the emperor greeted foreign emissaries at is called the _____.

2. The _____ is a famous Shinto shrine that was founded in the place where legend says a Japanese god appeared riding a deer.

3. Emperor Shomu ordered the construction of _____ throughout Japan.

4. The first Japanese books are history books called _____ and the _____.

5. The capital of Japan during the Nara period was called _____.

6. _____ moved the capital of Japan to Heiankyo, which ended the Nara period.

Chapter 6: The Heian Period

The Heian period is the sixth and final period of Ancient Japanese history, lasting from 794 CE to 1185 CE. That's 391 years! It's the longest historical period we've seen since the Yayoi period. This time had a lot of political fighting and economic failure, but it also made important cultural contributions. In fact, the culture that started during the Heian Period is still a big part of Japanese culture today.

The Byōdō-In Temple, 11th century (https://flic.kr/p/hw2tKU)

Historians say the Heian period started in 794 CE because that's when Emperor Kanmu moved the capital of Japan from Nara to Heiankyo. Did you know that "Heian" means "peace" in English? Some historians think that Emperor Kanmu named the new capital after peace because he hoped it would help settle things down. Emperor Kanmu left Nara because the political fighting had gotten bad. He was frustrated that even the Buddhist priests were fighting for power in the government. So, he declared that he was moving the capital - but Heiankyo wasn't the first city he tried to move to.

Emperor Kanmu first tried to set up the new capital in Nagaokakyo, only a few miles away from Heiankyo. However, things went wrong right away - several people died, and Emperor Kanmu believed the city was cursed. If you believe in curses, they can be scary, and the Japanese people believed that curses had the power to hurt them. Emperor Kanmu decided to move the capital again to Heiankyo.

The new capital at Heiankyo was built like Nara had been. It had wide streets, a huge imperial palace, and Chinese-style buildings based on the Chinese Tang capital Chang'an. This new city was very successful. Heiankyo was the capital of Japan for about 1,000 years, and you can still visit it today as the modern city of Kyoto. There aren't any original parts of the imperial palace still standing because of earthquakes and fires, but the city is still growing.

The most important part of the Heian period was its art. This part of its history formed the basis of modern Japanese culture, and so much Japanese art and literature are still influenced by this period. The most exciting creation was Japan's first novel. Some historians even think it was the first novel in the world. It was written by Lady Murasaki Shikibu and called The Tale of Genji. Can you imagine writing the first novel ever? You would have to be imaginative to create a new type of storytelling.

Lady Murasaki Shikibu had a good imagination. She was also well educated because she was part of the aristocracy. Women in the aristocracy were taught about all forms of art. In addition to writing, Lady Shikibu also liked music and calligraphy (handwriting that is so pretty that the handwriting itself is art!)

The Tale of Genji tells the story of Prince Genji in the Heian imperial court. The story talks about his life and romantic relationships, and the book ends by telling the story of Genji's son, Kaoru. The whole story is fictional, but Lady Murasaki Shikibu showed the real parts of living in the imperial court.

Another important book that comes from the Heian period is The Pillow Book by Sei Shōnagon. Sei Shōnagon lived at the same time as Lady Murasaki Shikibu, and they knew each other well. Sei Shōnagon became part of the imperial court in 993 CE, and her book reads like a diary. Your diary might be private, but Sei Shōnagon's book quickly became public. The Pillow Book talks about life in the imperial court, and

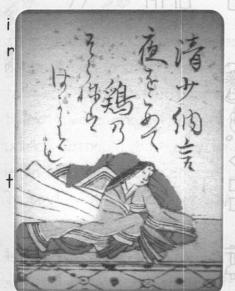

many of her stories are funny. (There isn't one set story; instead, the book ambles from one topic to the next, which is why it reads so much like a diary.) Historians particularly like The Pillow Book because they can learn much about the life and behaviors of the aristocracy during this time.

Sei Shōnagon, illustration:
(https://commons.wikimedia.org
/wiki/File:Hyakuninisshu_062.jpg#/media/
File:Hyakuninisshu_062.jpg)

Other types of art were also popular during the Heian period, including poetry, painting, and sculpting. The sculptures and paintings often centered around Buddhism. New sects (varieties) of Buddhism appeared in Japan, and the artwork of the period helped spread the new sects' ideas across the island.

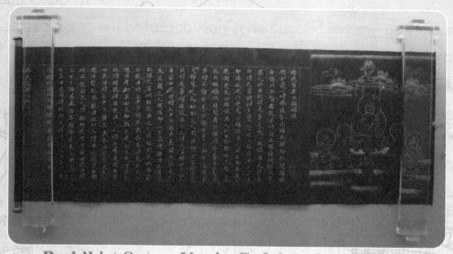

Buddhist Sutra, Kenja Gofukutoku, 1185:
(https://commons.wikimedia.org/wiki/File:Kenja_gofukutoku_kyo_
Sutra,_1185,_Tokyo_National_Museum.JPG#/media/File:Kenja_
gofukutoku_kyo_Sutra,_1185,_Tokyo_National_Museum.JPG)

Although the people in Japan's aristocracy enjoyed making art, the rest of the country experienced hard times during the Heian period. The imperial court was so busy taking care of itself that it couldn't care for the common people. Emperor Kanmu tried to help, so he made changes to the government, such as lowering taxes, and he also tried to conquer the Emishi people who lived in northern Japan. The Emishi people fought with the emperors for years, and Emperor Kanmu was ready to be finished with it all!

So, he created a new government position called the Seiitai-Shogun. Eventually, this role became the Shogun, one man who was very powerful during the times of the samurai warriors. When the position was first created, it wasn't made for the best warrior of society. Instead, he was just the general in charge of conquest. Sakanoue no Tamuramaro was the Shogun who finally defeated the Emishi people. He expanded the imperial court's power into Northern Japan.

While Sakanoue no Tamuramaro was fighting in Northern Japan, the imperial court was being torn apart by political fighting. The Fujiwara clan grabbed power by manipulating (tricking) the emperors. Other powerful families were angry that the Fujiwara clan was taking all the power for themselves.

All this fighting for control over the imperial court kept the government too busy to notice they were losing control of the rural areas of Japan. Most people lived in rural areas (the countryside) in these times, and because these places were far from the imperial court, the nobility began to collect land. They put their land together into large manors and made the local farmers live and work on the manors. As the manors got bigger and bigger, the nobility needed help protecting them, so they started to employ personal armies. Instead of the army reporting to the general or the emperor, each army reported to a nobleman. These private armies eventually became the samurai that were popular in later periods in Japan.

The Fujiwara clan had power for most of the Heian period, but two other clans challenged them near the end. These two clans were the

Minamoto clan and the Taira clan. These two clans used armies of samurai warriors to overthrow the Fujiwara clan, but then they started fighting with each other.

Genpei Kassen

(https://commons.wikimedia.org/wiki/File:Genpei_kassen.jpg#/media/File:Genpei_kassen.jpg)

The Minamoto clan and the Taira clan fought several wars. The last one was called the Genpei War, and it lasted from 1180 CE to 1185 CE. The Minamoto clan beat the Taira clan, and the Minamoto clan quickly took control of the government. Yoritomo, the Minamoto clan leader, was made Shogun by the emperor shortly after the Genpei War was over.

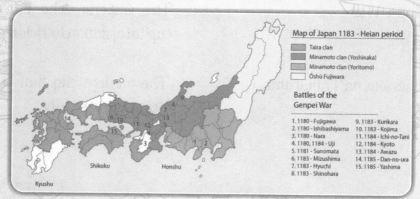

Map of Japan in 1183, Heian Period during the Genpei war

The Heian Period had a lot of political fighting, and it ended with a war between two clans who wanted political power. Although it was probably a little scary to live during the Heian period, the culture of this period lives on. It started the samurai culture, and it changed Japanese art in ways that are still a part of Japanese culture today.

Chapter 6: Challenge

Can you match the word or person with the correct description?

1. Kyoto

   a. Author of The Tale of Genji

2. Sei Shōnagon

   b. The war that ended the Heian period

3. Emperor Kanmu

   c. The Shogun who defeated the Emishi people in northern Japan

4. Lady Murasaki Shikibu

   d. Author of The Pillow Book

5. Genpei War

   e. The emperor who moved the capital of Japan to Heiankyo

6. Sakanoue no Tamuramaro

   f. The modern city that is where Heiankyo used to be

Chapter 7: Famous Historical Figures

Throughout ancient Japanese history, we've met a lot of important people. Some of those people were emperors, some were soldiers, and some were writers. In this chapter, we will learn more about eight of the most important people in ancient Japanese history. Of course, these people are not the only important people in Japanese history, but they are a great place to start. So, get ready to dive in and learn about how each one of them changed ancient Japanese history.

Empress Suiko (554-628 CE)

Empress Suiko was the first empress (female ruler) in Ancient Japanese history. She was also the first woman in Eastern Asia to have so much power in her country's government. She selected Prince Shotoku to be her regent because he was very smart and was good at running the government.

Empress Suiko loved the arts, but she also really wanted to take care of her people. During her reign, she ordered the construction of roads in Japan to help people move products across the country. This was particularly helpful for farmers and messengers, but the roads helped everyone. She also helped the farmers develop new ways to water their crops, leading to more food for the people and better taxes coming in for the imperial court.

Empress Suiko cared deeply about the people of Japan. Everything she did was meant to help them, and she is best remembered as the first great empress of Japan.

Empress Suiko (554 CE – 15 April 628 CE)
:(https://commons.wikimedia.org/wiki/File:Empress_Suiko_2.jpg#/media/File:Empress_Suiko_2.jpg)

Prince Shotoku (574 - 622 CE)

Prince Shotoku is best remembered for spreading Buddhism throughout Japan and for restructuring the government. He ruled as regent for Empress Suiko, who was his aunt. She was more interested in art, so she let Prince Shotoku handle the political side of being emperor.

Prince Shotoku saw that the government during the Asuka period had a lot of corruption. Corrupt governments aren't good for anybody, so Prince Shotoku did his best to fix it. One of the big things he did to fix the government was to write a new constitution. It is called the Seventeen Article Constitution, and it had many laws that encouraged people to live in harmony with each other and to obey the emperor.

Prince Shotoku also was a big supporter of Buddhism. He built 46 different temples and monasteries in his lifetime all over Japan. That's a lot of temples! When Prince Shotoku died in 622 CE, the people of Japan were very sad. They mourned for him for a long time, and they also made him a Buddhist saint because he worked hard to create a good government for Japan.

Empress Gemmei (661-721 CE)

Empress Gemmei was the 43rd emperor of Japan. She came to the throne in 707 CE as the regent for her grandson, Emperor Shomu. Emperor Shomu was still a child, and running a country was a lot of responsibility for a child. So, Empress Gemmei ruled in his place to give him time to grow up.

Empress Gemmei is best remembered for moving the Japanese capital from Fujiwara to Nara. This move started the Nara period in 710 CE. Although the city was only the capital of Japan for about 84 years, it was built like the Chinese Tang capital and had many different Buddhist temples in it. Empress Gemmei retired from being emperor in 715 CE. She allowed her daughter, Empress Genshō, to reign after her until Emperor Shomu became an adult and could rule Japan on his own.

Empress Gemmei (707-715 CE):

(https://commons.wikimedia.org/wiki/File:Empress_Gemmei.jpg#/media/File:Empress_Gemmei.jpg)

Emperor Kanmu is best remembered for moving the capital of Japan from Nara to Heiankyo. This move ended the Nara period and started the Heian period - this means he was an emperor in two different historical periods! Emperor Kanmu wanted to move the capital because he wanted to get away from some of the corruption in Nara.

Emperor Kanmu did not like politicians taking advantage of the government (or the peasants) to get power. Can you imagine living in a world where government officials only worked to help themselves instead of helping other people?

Emperor Kanmu didn't have to imagine it. Although the first thing he did was move the capital, Emperor Kanmu also took other steps to make sure that the government ran like it was supposed to.

As emperor, he was supposed to have all the power to run things how he wanted to. Emperor Kanmu began to cut down the royal court because

Emperor Kammu (781 to 806 CE):

smaller groups are usually cheaper and easier to deal with. He also took care of the peasants in Japan by lowering taxes and allowing them to focus on farming. Many historians think that Emperor Kanmu was a great emperor because he took care of his people and reduced corruption in the ancient Japanese government.

Sakanoue no Tamuramaro (758-811 CE)

Sakanoue no Tamuramaro was a great military leader during the Heian period. He quickly rose through the military ranks to the position of Vice Commander and did most of his military work in the northern parts of Japan. In 797 CE, Sakanoue no Tamuramaro was given the title of Seiitai Shōgun. He was the first man ever to have the job, and his first task was to take all northern Japan for the emperor.

To do that, he had to fight the Emishi people. They had been living in northern Japan for centuries, and these people were led by chief commanders, Aterui and More. Although Sakanoue no Tamuramaro defeated the Emishi people, he greatly respected Aterui and More because they were good military leaders.

After his success, Sakanoue no Tamuramaro built several castles and temples. Many of his castles were built in northern Japan. This is a way for a conquering people, like the Japanese, to make sure everyone knows they are in charge. Sakanoue no Tamuramaro eventually died in 811 CE, but he is still remembered today as a great warrior and hero.

Fujiwara no Michinaga (966-1027 CE)

Fujiwara no Michinaga was one of the most powerful imperial court politicians during the Heian Period. Think for a moment about how you would gain power with a king or an emperor. How would you do it? You might try doing them a favor or becoming friends, but you might also try to make a family connection. Fujiwara no Michinaga did just that—he made sure that his daughter married Emperor Ichijo.

Eventually, Fujiwara no Michinaga's grandson was emperor. Because Fujiwara no Michinaga was Emperor Goichijo's grandfather, he had a lot of power. In fact, he had so much power that no one in the imperial court dared to say anything bad about him. That's a LOT of power! Fujiwara no Michinaga was the most powerful person in the Fujiwara clan, and he helped run the government during the Heian period.

Sei Shōnagon (966-1025 CE)

Sei Shōnagon was a writer during the Heian Period and the author of The Pillow Book. This book contains the best descriptions of imperial court life during the Heian Period, and it is also a piece of classic Japanese literature.

The Pillow Book is still popular today because Sei Shōnagon was witty, which means that she could say funny things in response to almost anything. Sei Shōnagon was part of the imperial court from 993 to 1000 CE, and she directly served Empress Teishi because she was both funny and intelligent.

Unfortunately, historians do not know much more about Sei Shōnagon other than what she writes in The Pillow Book. Her book is one of the best examples of a diary-style book, and it is still read and enjoyed by people around the world today.

Murasaki Shikibu is the author of Japan's first novel, The Tale of Genji. She wrote this book while she was part of the imperial court during the Heian period. She served Empress Akiko, and she was part of the court at the same time as Sei Shōnagon. Sadly, though, the two women writers did not like each other. In fact, Murasaki Shikibu wrote in her diary about how much she did not like Sei Shōnagon!

Historians do not know much about her other than what Murasaki Shikibu told us in her novel, diary, and poetry. They do know that she was part of the Fujiwara family. They also know that she liked to play the harp, paint, and write calligraphy. Other than that, we know very little; we don't even know when she died! Historians think she died sometime after 1013 CE, but no one is sure exactly when.

Murasaki Shikibu (978—1014 CE)
(https://commons.wikimedia.org/wiki/File:Murasaki-Shikibu-composing-Genji
-Monogatari.png#/media/File:Murasaki-Shikibu-composing-Genji-Monogatari.png)

Can you fill in the blank for each of these sentences with one of the words below?

Fujiwara no Michinaga		Sakanoue no Tamuramaro
Empress Gemmei	Murasaki Shikibu	Prince Shotoku
Sei Shōnagon	Empress Suiko	Emperor Kanmu

1. _____ was one of the most powerful politicians during the Heian period.

2. _____ was the first empress in Ancient Japanese history.

3. The first novel is called The Tale of Genji, and it was written by _____.

4. After moving the capital of Japan from Nara to Heiankyo, _____ got rid of a lot of corruption in the government.

5. _____ wrote the Seventeen Article Constitution during the Asuka period.

6. The first person to be given the title of Shogun was _____.

7. The author of The Pillow Book was _____.

8. _____ moved the capital of Japan from Fujiwara to Nara.

Chapter 8: Culture and Society

So far, we have learned about some historical events that shaped ancient Japanese history. We have talked about wars and famous people, but history is more than just all that. History is also about the way people lived their lives, which historians call culture and society.

Culture is all the art that people make and live with. Society is how people normally live and how they interact with each other. In this chapter, we're going to focus on those - so get ready to be amazed by the art and lives of the ancient Japanese people.

Each person experiences society and culture differently depending on their social class. Poorer people don't get to use and enjoy as much art as people who are in the ruling class. This was true in ancient Japan. Although Japan did have a lot of art and culture, the people who enjoyed it the most were the aristocrats - higher up the ladder. The poorer people lived very hard lives; their homes were small and cold, and they were often hungry. They also suffered from several pandemics (widespread sickness), and a lot of people died because they didn't understand how germs work back then. If you were not part of the ruling class, you would have lived a hard life in ancient Japan.

Because the ruling class had nicer houses and more food, they could enjoy and create culture. The first signs of art in ancient Japan came from its pottery. The Japanese people invented pottery during the

Jōmon period. This pottery was usually simple and black, and it was decorated by pressing rope into the wet clay to leave markings and patterns. As the Jōmon period continued, these decorations got prettier. Then, the Yayoi period came, and they had a different type of pottery; their pottery was red or grey, but it was much less decorated than the Jōmon pottery.

Then came the Kofun period. Although the people during the Kofun period made pots and jars, they are more famous for making haniwa. Haniwa is little figurines made of pottery. They could be shaped like a person, a house, or even an animal. Horse figurines were popular during the Kofun time.

Haniwa Warrior in Keiko Armor, Kofun Period, 6th Century
(https://flic.kr/p/FAXQjH)

Although you might think that they made the haniwa as toys, the ancient Japanese made them decorate their tombs, and remember, the tombs of the Kofun period were really important to their culture. They built the tombs to look like keyholes, and some of these keyhole-shaped tombs are bigger than a football field. The haniwa stood outside the tomb, guarding all around it.

Kofun Period Haniwa Terracotta Building (https://flic.kr/p/FB3pAp)

But the haniwa wasn't the only art that the people living in the Kofun period put in their tombs. They also put bronze mirrors, armor, swords, and jewelry. Can you imagine why people would bury all this art and treasure in their tombs? It makes it hard for other people to enjoy the art because they can't see it. Historians don't know why the ancient Japanese people buried so much art in their tombs during the Kofun period. Until they figure it out, we can still enjoy all the art that has been found.

Kofun Period Necklaces (https://flic.kr/p/FAQNUJ)

The next period of ancient Japanese history was the Asuka period. Pottery continued to get better quickly. Artists began to use a pottery wheel instead of making everything by hand, but pottery wasn't the only kind of art that became popular. So many types of art became popular that artists were given tax breaks so that they could focus on making more art. Literature and music were very popular during the Asuka period, but when Buddhism became popular, the people found another type of art to enjoy - building temples.

Did you know that even buildings can be art? Although most buildings are built to be useful, some buildings are also designed to be beautiful. During the Asuka period, people were very concerned with creating very pretty temples. Each was built with local supplies, and the builders made sure that each beam and shingle was in the perfect spot. Everything was based on horizontal and vertical lines. They also made sure the buildings around the temple were put in the right places, so the whole grounds around were part of the temple. After it was built, the artists of the Asuka period made bronze and wooden sculptures of the Buddha, which helped complete the whole building.

The love of art continued into the Nara period. The people continued to build beautiful temples, including the Daibutsuden; this is the biggest wooden building in the world, and it holds the Great Buddha, which is the biggest bronze statue of the Buddha ever made! The people of the Nara period were religious, and their faith shows through in their culture and art. Culture always shows what the people of a time were most concerned about, so studying the culture can help you better understand history - and the people.

The first history of Japan comes from the Nara period, and it is called the Nihon Shoki. This book was written by a group of scholars and was finished in 720 CE. Did you know that a lot of history books are written by a group of people? Writing with a group helps to keep everyone honest, which makes the history more correct. The Nihon Shoki is different from our history books today because it includes a lot of mythology. Myths are fictional stories that are important to a culture, so all the myths included in the Nihon Shoki were important to the ancient Japanese people. The book also includes many facts, which is where historians learn so much about ancient Japan.

The love of books and literature continued into the Heian period. Murasaki Shikibu wrote the first novel ever; she was part of the imperial court and was very educated. Her novel is called The Tale of Genji.

Scenes from the Tale of Genji: The Sacred Tree
(https://commons.wikimedia.org/w/index.php?search=The+Sacred+Tree+from+The+Tale+of+Genji&title=Special:
MediaSearch&go=Go&type=image)

The novel tells the story of Prince Genji, who is a perfect gentleman in every way. The story tells all about his life in the imperial court during the Heian period as he looks for love and success.

Scenes from the Tale of Genji: Butterflies

The other famous book from the Heian period is called The Pillow Book by Sei Shonagon. She was also part of the imperial court, but her book is more like a diary. Sei Shonagon wrote down many of her thoughts and observations about the imperial court, and she often tells funny stories. She also lists things that she thought were interesting, just like you might do in your own diary. This writing style is called a rambling style, and The Pillow Book is one of the first books to use the rambling style in Japanese history. It is also one of the best.

Other forms of art, such as painting and calligraphy, influenced the culture of Ancient Japan, and art continues to change Japanese culture today. As society becomes easier for people of all social classes, more people can be part of the culture, so more people are making art.

Chapter 8: Challenge

Can you match the word or person with the correct description?

1. Culture

   a. Pottery figurines that were placed around tombs during the Kofun period

2. Society

   b. The Asuka temple where the Great Buddha is

3. Sei Shonagon

   c. The first history book of Ancient Japan

4. Nihon Shoki

   d. All the art that people make and live with

5. Haniwa

   e. The first novel in the world

6. The Tale of Genji

   f. How people normally live and interact with each other

7. Daibutsuden

   g. Author of The Pillow Book

Chapter 9: Myths and Legends

Mythology is important to every culture. These are the fictional stories that people tell themselves about their background, beliefs, and their world. Often, these stories involve deities and unbelievable events. Deities is another word for gods.

This is all true of the ancient Japanese myth; we'll explore some of the most popular myths from ancient Japan in this chapter. Get ready to learn about how the island of Japan was pulled out of the sea and how the emperors themselves come from the gods above. While it might not all be historical, it's still fun to read about!

The god Izanagi and goddess Izanami
(https://commons.wikimedia.org/wiki/File:Kobayashi_
Izanami_and_Izanagi.jpg#/media/File:Kobayashi_
Izanami_and_Izanagi.jpg)

Let's start by meeting the main deities. Izanagi and Izanami were the first two gods. Izanagi is the father of all things, and Izanami is the mother of all things. Before they started working, there was nothing but chaos. Can you imagine a world where nothing exists? There wouldn't be any people or land or stars.

Izanagi and Izanami wanted to fix that by creating everything in the world. Together, they made the first island of Japan by stirring the sea with their divine spear. The water that dripped from the spear formed the islands. The two gods then got married and began to have children. Their children would become the other islands of Japan and the other deities.

Sadly, Izanami died giving birth. Izanagi was so upset that he tried to get her back from Yomi, (the underworld), but he could not bring her back. She had eaten the food from Yomi, and so she could never leave. Izanagi was very upset because he had lost his wife. Once he escaped, he went to bathe, and his bath produced the last three deities.

These gods would end up being some of the most important gods in Japanese mythology. They are Amaterasu, Susanoo, and Tsukuyomi. Amaterasu is the goddess of the sun. She would take her father's place as the ruler of all the gods, and she was the most beautiful goddess of them all. Susanoo is the god of the sea and storms. He liked to play tricks on the others and is known for being chaotic. Tsukuyomi is the god of the moon, and he stands for order. He is separated from Amaterasu and spends the whole day chasing after her in the sky.

Now that you have met all the most important deities from Japanese mythology, let's look at some of their stories. These stories mostly come from the Nihon Shoki, which is the first Japanese history book. It also had a lot of mythology in it. Many of the myths are also told in the Kojiki, which is another ancient Japanese history book. If you want to read the original stories, you can read these two books about these myths and legends.

The Sun, the Moon, and the Wind

At first, the three siblings, Amaterasu, Susanoo, and Tsukuyomi, all got along. But if you have siblings, you know that sometimes fighting happens. If you have divine fights, though, the consequences are bigger.

Amaterasu and Tsukuyomi had a fight so big that it created day and night. In the beginning, they were best friends. It seemed like nothing would ever separate them, which meant that the sun and the moon were in the sky at the same time, so there was no separation between day and night. Can you imagine that?

Tsukuyomi-no-Mikoto, Shinto Moon God

(https://commons.wikimedia.org/wiki/File:Shinto
-Tsukuyomi-no-Mikoto-Old-
Artwork.png#/media/File:Shinto-Tsukuyomi-no-
Mikoto-Old-Artwork.png)

One day, Amaterasu was invited to a party by Uke Mochi, the goddess of food. She couldn't go, so she let Tsukuyomi go instead. At first, he had a great time, but then he learned how Uke Mochi was making all the food. Instead of cooking it in a kitchen as we would, she threw it up (vomited) and then served it to the gods. It was gross! Tsukuyomi was so disgusted that he killed Uke Mochi. That made Amaterasu upset, which we can understand. As punishment, she banished Tsukuyomi from her palace. Banishing people means throwing them out and never letting them come back. The separation between Amaterasu and Tsukuyomi created day and night.

Amaterasu also had fights with Susanoo. He was jealous that she was the leader of the gods because he wanted to be the leader. He often played tricks on the other gods, and his tricks weren't always nice - probably because he was the god of storms and the sea. Both of these things can be chaotic, and Susanoo liked making chaos. But he was bitter that the other gods liked Amaterasu more (because she didn't play mean tricks on anybody!)

So, one day, he challenged her to a contest. Whoever could create more deities would win the contest. Amaterasu took his sword and made three deities, and Susanoo took her necklace and made five deities. At first, Susanoo thought he had won. It looks that way, doesn't it? But Amaterasu pointed out that she actually made the five deities because she had given him the necklace. She won the contest. This made Susanoo very angry, and he destroyed most of her palace before leaving in a rage.

Susanoo would eventually calm down, and he even married a beautiful woman after saving her from an evil dragon. The dragon was named

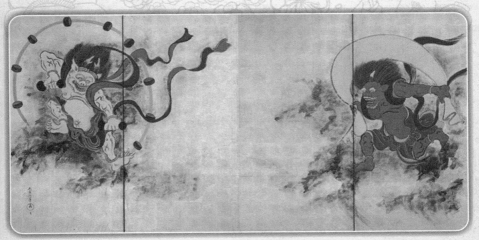

Susanoo, Wind God

Orochi, and it had eight heads. Susanoo tricked the dragon into drinking so much sake (Japanese wine) that it was drunk. Then, he defeated the dragon and married his wife. He even made up with his sister by giving her the special sword hidden in the dragon's tail.

Amaterasu and the Cave

Do you remember when Susanoo destroyed most of Amaterasu's palace in his anger over losing a contest? Well, Amaterasu was really upset by that. In fact, she was so upset that she ran away and hid in a cave. Because she was the sun goddess, she took the sun with her into the cave, and the rest of the world suffered in darkness. Everything began to die, and the other gods decided they needed her to come out of the cave. Although they asked nicely, she refused to come out.

Finally, the gods decided to trick her into coming out. This wasn't a trick like Susanoo used to play; instead, it was a nice trick. The gods put a mirror in front of the cave and then threw a big party. Amaterasu heard everyone having a good time with music, dancing, and laughter. It

Amaterasu, the Japanese Sun goddess
(https://commons.wikimedia.org/wiki/File:Amaterasu_cave_-_large_-_1856.jpeg#/media/
File:Amaterasu_cave_-_large_-_1856.jpeg)

was enough to make anyone curious. Amaterasu peaked out of the cave and saw her reflection in the mirror. She was amazed at her own reflection and stepped out of the cave. Immediately, the sun came back, and the gods celebrated Amaterasu's return as their leader.

Emperor Jimmu

Many of the gods had children and grandchildren. Amaterasu had several children, and she sent her grandson Ninigi down to Earth to rule it. He also got married and had children. Eventually, Emperor Jimmu was born. He was human but was still related to the gods. This gave him the divine right to be the emperor of Japan, so he became the legendary first emperor of Japan. Legend says that he also started the Yamato dynasty, which still rules Japan today.

Chapter 9: Challenge

Can you fill in the blank for each of these sentences with one of the words below?

Amaterasu	cave	Susanoo	Tsukuyomi
Izanagi and Izanami		Emperor Jimmu	Yomi

1. _____ is the goddess of the sun.

2. _____ is the legendary first emperor of Japan.

3. _____ is the god of the moon.

4. _____ created everything in the world.

5. When Izanami died, she had to stay in _____ for all time because she had eaten the food of the underworld.

6. _____ is the god of the sea and storms.

7. Amaterasu hid in a _____ because she was upset about the mean tricks Susanoo played.

Chapter 10: Religion and Spirituality

Did you know that there are a lot of different religions in the world? Religion is a belief in and worship of a God (one god) or gods (different gods). It is usually concerned about how people should live and how people can connect to the spirit world. That's called spirituality. Every culture has its own religions, and the two big religions in ancient Japan were Shinto and Buddhism.

Shinto was the only religion in Japan from the Jōmon period until the end of the Kofun period. Shinto is based on mythology from the last chapter. The people who believe in Shinto believe in Izanagi, Izanami, Amaterasu, Susanoo, and Tsukuyomi. Of course, all these myths developed over time as people told them over and over again - they didn't just appear one day!

Religion during the Jōmon and Yayoi periods was not organized. We know they had figurines of deities, which they called kami, and that they had festivals. Their worship of the kami was focused on nature because they needed good harvests to survive. Because they didn't understand the science of farming, the early people of Japan relied on shamans. Shamans are the people who have access and some control over spirits in the spirit world. Through magic or prayers, shamans can make the spirits do things that help people on Earth. Not everyone today believes that shamans have this power, but the ancient Japanese people believed it very much.

Shinto continues today in Japan. It focuses on respecting nature and your ancestors. But Shinto is not the only religion in Japan. At the end of the Kofun period, Buddhism was introduced to Japan. In 604 CE,

Prince Shotoku made Buddhism the country's religion, so Buddhism spread to Japan's people. By making Buddhism Japan's religion, Prince Shotoku told everyone that they had to convert to Buddhism. Can you imagine living in a world where you had to believe in a specific religion? You might think it limits your freedoms, or you might enjoy knowing that everyone believes the same things you do.

Buddha at birth (Asuka Period): (https://commons.wikimedia.org/wiki/File:Buddha _at_birth_(Tanjobutsu),_Japan,_Asuka_period,_600 s_AD,_gilt_bronze_-_Freer_Gallery_of_Art_- DSC04782.jpg)

We don't know how the ancient Japanese felt about becoming Buddhist. Many common people still believed in Shinto, but Buddhism was more popular in the imperial court. So, both religions existed at the same time. Some people probably even believed in both religions, even though Buddhism was the official religion of Japan. Buddhism influenced many artists, so a lot of the art we have from ancient Japan is sculptures of the Buddha. Temple building was especially popular during the Asuka period and the Nara period and the temples were also works of art.

Because Buddhism was important to the imperial court, many Buddhist monks got used to having money and power. Power corrupts -making

you choose wrongly and unfairly - especially if you aren't careful. The Buddhist monks were so focused on getting power that they stopped focusing on Buddhism and instead focused on the government! Of course, not all Buddhist monks were like this. Some really wanted to bring peace to everyone and help everyone get enlightenment. Sadly, there were enough monks who were only focused on themselves, which corrupted the Buddhist priesthood during the Nara and Heian periods.

The people of Japan didn't like that bad monks corrupted the Buddhist priesthood. They felt that Buddhism needed to be fixed or reformed. Two good monks went to China to learn more about Buddhism so that they could reform the religion. Their names were Kukai and Sachio. Both men returned to Japan and founded new temples that had different teachings. These different teachings within Buddhism are called sects, which means that there are different groups of people within a religion. They all believe in the same basic religion, but important differences between each group make them special.

Kukai founded the Shingon sect. His sect focused on making Buddhism easy for the common people to learn and participate in. Shingon Buddhism is all about artwork, chanting, and specific yoga poses. Although you can do yoga for exercise, some people also do it as part of their religion. The common people liked this sect of Buddhism because they could do the right things and get enlightenment. They didn't have to give up their farms or their families to be good Buddhists.

Sachio founded the second Buddhist sect called Tendai. Tendai taught that there was only one really important scripture called the Lotus Sutra. The Lotus Sutra says that anyone can get enlightenment if they focus only on this teaching. If a person focuses just right, that person can even get to Nirvana, which Buddhists believe is the best place to go once you die. The Lotus Sutra is easy to understand, so people who believed in the Tendai sect of Buddhism would focus on the Lotus Sutra only. It was only one thing, so Tendai was also popular with the common people. They only had to learn one sutra, and it was easy to understand without making their lives harder.

Nara Period - A Preaching Buddha:
(https://commons.wikimedia.org/wiki/File:Japan,_Nara_Period_-_A_Preaching_Buddha_-_1985.87_-_Cleveland_Museum_of_Art.jpg#/media/File:Japan,_Nara_Period_-_A_Preaching_Buddha_-_1985.87_-_Cleveland_Museum_of_Art.jpg)

During the Heian period, Buddhism was popular in Japan. Shinto and Buddhism were practiced together for a brief time, but that stopped as Buddhism became more popular with the imperial court. Just like before, many Buddhist monks became corrupted because powerful aristocrats surrounded them. The monks liked having lots of power and money, and they started focusing on that instead of on Buddhism. As Buddhist monks became more corrupt, the common people stopped being interested in Buddhism. Most people don't like being part of bad groups, and corrupt groups aren't good for anyone. It wasn't until the very end of the Heian period that Buddhism became easier for everyone to be part of.

The corruption fell apart with the end of the Heian period because of the big political changes, like the Gempei War, and Buddhism was popular again with the Japanese people.

Japan, Heian period (A.D. 794 - 1185) (https://flic.kr/p/Hc9LmK)

The history of Ancient Japan is rich. It is filled with interesting men and women who developed their own cultures, myths, and religions.

We have met their warrior empresses, and we have learned about the special tombs they built. We have read their mythology and learned how Japan was created from a drop of water falling off a divine spear. We have even met some of the Japanese artists who invented pottery and wrote the first novel.

We hope you have enjoyed getting an up-close view of ancient Japanese history. The Japanese people have always been innovative, and their innovations so long ago continue to impact all of us today!

Chapter 10: Challenge

Can you match the word or person with the correct description?

1. Sachio

a. The religion that focuses on respecting nature and your ancestors

2. Shamans

b. Made the Tendai Buddhist sect

3. Shinto

c. The name for the Japanese gods

4. Kukai

d. People who use magic or prayers to control the spirit world

5. Lotus Sutra

e. Made the Shingon Buddhist sect

6. Kami

f. The most important teaching of the Tendai Buddhist sect

If you want to learn more about tons of other exciting historical periods, check out our other books!

ANCIENT HISTORY
FOR KIDS

A CAPTIVATING GUIDE TO ANCIENT GREECE, ROME, AND EGYPT FOR CHILDREN

CAPTIVATING HISTORY

BIBLIOGRAPHY

If you want to learn more about ancient Japanese history, check out these websites and videos!

Ancient Civilizations: The Illustrated Guide to Belief, Mythology, and Art. Professor Greg Wolf, 2005

Ancient China by Dale Anderson, 2005.

Exploring Ancient China by Elaine Landau, 2005.

Celebrate Chinese New Year: With Fireworks, Dragons, and Lanterns by Carolyn Otto, 2009

https://www.ducksters.com/history/china/ancient_china.php

https://www.dkfindout.com/us/history/ancient-china/

https://www.historyforkids.net/history-of-china.html

https://kids.nationalgeographic.com/pages/article/chinese-horoscopes

Ancient Japanese mythology. *Mythopedia*. 2019. https://mythopedia.com/japanese-mythology/.

"Asuka Period." *Academic Kids Encyclopedia*. Accessed Sep. 2021. https://academickids.com/encyclopedia/index.php/Asuka_period.

"Asuka Period Facts for Kids." *Kiddle Encyclopedia*. July 2021. https://kids.kiddle.co/Asuka_period.

Cartwright, Mark. "Ancient Japan." *World History Encyclopedia*. UNESCO Archives. June 2017. https://www.worldhistory.org/Ancient_Japan/.

– –. "Asuka Period." *World History Encyclopedia*. UNESCO Archives. April 2017. https://www.worldhistory.org/Asuka_Period/.

– –. "Emperor Kammu." *World History Encyclopedia*. UNESCO Archives. May 2017. https://www.worldhistory.org/Emperor_Kammu/.

– –. "Heian Period." *World History Encyclopedia*. UNESCO Archives. May 2017. https://www.worldhistory.org/Heian_Period/.

— -. "Nara Period." *World History Encyclopedia*. UNESCO Archives. April 2017. https://www.worldhistory.org/Nara_Period/.

— -. "Nihon Shoki." *World History Encyclopedia*. UNESCO Archives. May 2017. https://www.worldhistory.org/Nihon_Shoki/.

— -. "Prince Shotoku." *World History Encyclopedia*. UNESCO Archives. June 2017. https://www.worldhistory.org/Prince_Shotoku/.

— -. "Tale of Genji." *World History Encyclopedia*. UNESCO Archives. April 2017. https://www.worldhistory.org/Tale_of_Genji/.

— -. "The Pillow Book." *World History Encyclopedia*. UNESCO Archives. April 2017. https://www.worldhistory.org/The_Pillow_Book/.

Coman, Dr. Sonia. "Asuka Period, an Introduction." Khan Academy. 2021. https://www.khanacademy.org/humanities/art-asia/art-japan/x97ec695a:asuka-period/a/asuka-period-an-introduction.

"Empress Gemmei of Japan." *Academic Kids Encyclopedia*. Accessed Sep. 2021. http://academickids.com/encyclopedia/index.php/Empress_Gemmei_of_Japan.

Farris, William Wayne. "Daily Life and Demographics in Ancient Japan." *Michigan Monograph Series in Japanese Studies* 63. University of Michigan Press. 2009. https://www.press.umich.edu//9340257.

"Fujiwara Michinaga." *Your Dictionary*. Accessed Sep. 2021. https://biography.yourdictionary.com/fujiwara-michinaga.

"Heian Period." *Academic Kids Encyclopedia*. Accessed Sep. 2021. https://academickids.com/encyclopedia/index.php/Heian_period.

"Heian Period Facts for Kids." *Kiddle Encyclopedia*. Sep. 2021. https://kids.kiddle.co/Heian_period.

"Heijo Palace." Japan-Guide.com. July 2020. https://www.japan-guide.com/e/e4111.html.

"History of Japan Explained in Eight Minutes (All Periods of Japanese History Documentary)." YouTube video. Posted by Epimetheus. July 14, 2018. https://www.youtube.com/watch?v=rxQcQ5DJqqE&ab_channel=Epimetheu.

Hoang, Tony. "Yayoi Period." *World History Encyclopedia.* UNESCO Archives. March 2016. https://www.worldhistory.org/Yayoi_Period/.

"Japan in the Heian Period and Cultural History: Crash Course World History 227." YouTube video. Posted by CrashCourse. March 4, 2015. https://www.youtube.com/watch?v=ZnZEoOJ-cxE&ab_channel=CrashCourse.

"Japanese History: The Heian Period Pt. 1 (Japanese History: The Textbook)." YouTube video. Posted by Buyuuden Japanese History. July 16, 2021. https://www.youtube.com/watch?v=mF9RycAkYnk&ab_channel=BuyuudenJapaneseHistory.

"Japanese History: The Kofun Period (Japanese History: The Textbook Ep. 3)."

YouTube video. Posted by Buyuuden Japanese History. Feb. 28, 2021. https://www.youtube.com/watch?v=ZyjaCRGAqvA&ab_channel=BuyuudenJapaneseHistory.

"Japanese History: The Jomon Period (Japanese History: The Textbook Ep.1)." YouTube video. Posted by Buyuuden Japanese History. Feb. 6, 2021. https://www.youtube.com/watch?v=ha34-NIuM-U&t=155s&ab_channel=BuyuudenJapaneseHistory.

"Japanese History: The Nara Period Pt. 1 (Japanese History: The Textbook)." YouTube video. Posted by Buyuuden Japanese History. May 2, 2021. https://www.youtube.com/watch?v=GO9zUSJ8Xrs&ab_channel=BuyuudenJapaneseHistory.

"Japanese History: The Nara Period Pt. 2 (Japanese History: The Textbook)." YouTube video. Posted by Buyuuden Japanese History. May 28, 2021. https://www.youtube.com/watch?v=TGI3WtHJLNQ&ab_channel=BuyuudenJapaneseHistory.

"Japanese History: The Yayoi Period (Japanese History: The Textbook Ep. 2)." YouTube video. Posted by Buyuuden Japanese History. Feb. 15, 2021. https://www.youtube.com/watch?v=o87YkMtFjoE&ab_channel=BuyuudenJapaneseHistory.

"Jimmu." *Encyclopaedia Britannica.* March 2016. https://www.britannica.com/topic/Jimmu.

"Jomon." *Academic Kids Encyclopedia*. Accessed Sep. 2021. https://academickids.com/encyclopedia/index.php/Jomon.

"Jomon Culture." Jomon Japan. Accessed Sep. 2021. https://jomon-japan.jp/en/jomon-cultur/.

"Jōmon Period Facts for Kids." *Kiddle Encyclopedia*. July 2021. https://kids.kiddle.co/J%C5%8Dmon_period.

"Jomon, Yayoi, Kofun Period | Japanese Art History | Little Art Talks." YouTube video. Posted by Little Art Talks. Aug. 25, 2015. https://www.youtube.com/watch?v=hBs3aFM3cjM&ab_channel=LittleArtTalks.

"Kofun." *Academic Kids Encyclopedia*. Accessed Sep. 2021. https://academickids.com/encyclopedia/index.php/Kofun.

"Kofun Period Facts for Kids." *Kiddle Encyclopedia*. July 2021. https://kids.kiddle.co/Kofun_period.

Matsumoto, Nobuhiro. "Japanese mythology." *Encyclopaedia Britannica*. March 2007. https://www.britannica.com/topic/Japanese-mythology.

"Nara Period Facts for Kids." *Kiddle Encyclopedia*. July 2021. https://kids.kiddle.co/Nara_period.

"Sakanoue no Tamuramaro." *Japanese-Wiki-Corpus*. Japanese-English Bilingual Corpus of Wikipedia's Kyoto Articles with the National Institute of Information and Communications Technology. Accessed Sep. 2021. https://www.japanese-wiki-corpus.org/person/SAKANOUE%20no%20Tamuramaro.html.

Savage, George. "Japanese Pottery." *Encyclopaedia Britannica*. Oct. 2009. https://www.britannica.com/art/Japanese-pottery.

"Sei Shōnagon." *Encyclopaedia Britannica*. Jan. 2017. https://www.britannica.com/biography/Sei-Shonagon.

Symonds, Shannon Reed. "A History of Japanese Religion: From Ancient Times to Present" (2005). History Master's Theses. Paper 19. https://citeseerx.ist.psu.edu/viewdoc/download?doi=10.1.1.678.3045&rep=rep1&type=pdf.

"The Story of Empress Suiko." *Exploring the Footsteps of the Heroines of Asuka*. Asuka Japan Heritage Promotion Committee. Accessed Sep. 2021. https://asuka-japan-heritage.jp/global/en/suiko/life/.

Ulak, James T. "Japanese Architecture." *Encyclopaedia Britannica*. Sep. 2019. https://www.britannica.com/art/Japanese-architecture.

"Yayoi Period Facts for Kids." *Kiddle Encyclopedia*. July 2021. https://kids.kiddle.co/Yayoi_period.